ARE WE THERE YET?

Spiritual Explorations and Insights on Living in Happiness
on the Journey to Enlightenment

FELIX NTIFORO

BALBOA.
PRESS

A DIVISION OF HAY HOUSE

Balboa Press books may be ordered through booksellers or by contacting:

Balboa Press
A Division of Hay House
1663 Liberty Drive
Bloomington, IN 47403
www.balboapress.com
1 (877) 407-4847

Because of the dynamic nature of the Internet, any web addresses or links contained in this book may have changed since publication and may no longer be valid. The views expressed in this work are solely those of the author and do not necessarily reflect the views of the publisher, and the publisher hereby disclaims any responsibility for them.

The author of this book does not dispense medical advice or prescribe the use of any technique as a form of treatment for physical, emotional, or medical problems without the advice of a physician, either directly or indirectly. The intent of the author is only to offer information of a general nature to help you in your quest for emotional and spiritual well-being. In the event you use any of the information in this book for yourself, which is your constitutional right, the author and the publisher assume no responsibility for your actions.

Any people depicted in stock imagery provided by Thinkstock are models, and such images are being used for illustrative purposes only. Certain stock imagery © Thinkstock.

Print information available on the last page.

ISBN: 978-1-5043-8161-1 (sc)
ISBN: 978-1-5043-8163-5 (hc)
ISBN: 978-1-5043-8162-8 (e)

Library of Congress Control Number: 2017909385

Balboa Press rev. date: 07/19/2017

TABLE OF CONTENTS

There are many people in my life who have made contributions to accumulation of the ideas expressed in this book. Firstly I wish to thank my family for their continued support and encouragement. My daughter Tracy, for working many hours designing the cover, which is based on one of her extraordinary drawings. There are people with whom I have crossed paths over the years including friends, colleagues and former patients who were willing to spend time talking and mulling over ideas about life, and its influence on our growth as human beings. They have inspired me to get this book written.

INTRODUCTION: WALKING THE TALK

All I ever wanted was to be happy. I am 68 years old now and all I still want is to be happy. Does that mean then that maybe I haven't really changed at all? It bothered me for a while to realize that a part of me had not changed, and may never change. Maybe it is not supposed to change. For now, until I get to know better (and I hope I never do), I am growing to love this part of me. I am going to take a chance and believe there is an unchanging part of me that will always long for happiness, and that it is okay to be that way.

This is how life is. We are alive, we've been given the gift of life, and we are going to live. So, we may as well choose happiness.

This basic longing for happiness has led me through every episode in my life so far. I've been busy exploring as many methods of how to be happy as I can. Many of the techniques I've discovered were quite easy to mentally comprehend, but when it came to putting them into practice I kept running into problems. I'll start with the simplest principle I know, for an example, which is "Do not do anything to anybody that you would not like done to you." Have I paid attention to and practiced this principle most of the time? I must admit that until I realized how much discomfort I was causing myself by *not* following this rule, I was not even aware of how often I broke it! Even after I realized this was the root cause of many of my discomforts, doing something about it didn't always come easily. It meant tackling my issues about expectations and patience. I am pleased to say, though, that at this moment in time, at the ripe old age of 68, I am getting better at not breaking this rule as often as I used to. I can also say that I continue to feel better and better every day as I get better at working with love. Yes, I finally got the message behind this Golden Rule! It's about love.

Now I wake up every day anxious for an opportunity to help "transmit" love, and I don't feel the least bit selfish in admitting to the fact that the more love I help spread, the more love I get! Being filled with more love comes with the fringe benefit of feeling better and better! Apparently, there is no limit to it. I have heard this referred to as the "peace beyond all understanding" … but I am beginning to understand.

I am also slowly becoming aware of how simple it is to transmit love. Every moment seems to present a chance to do it, and I am getting better at being patient with myself. To borrow a baseball expression, my batting average is on the improve. How do I know that? Well, quite simply, every time I get a "hit" and succeed at being the best I can be in the moment, there is an explosion of light and sound within me – visible and audible love – and a jolt of happiness that leaves me feeling much better than I felt before. The only thing that interferes with my capacity to keep feeling better and better is my personal need for love. The needy me is my worst enemy. (Hence, perhaps, the phrase, "You are your own worst enemy.") I had a hard time coming to terms with the fact that I am basically the only one standing between me and God; that I am the one who is preventing myself from fully embracing life. Silly me! So, I decided to do something about this. That is when all the fun began, with the process of getting my self out of my own way.

I've found that the first and most easily accessible place to transmit love is in my thoughts. In my continuous attempts to discover practical ways to be happy, I learned from some sources that a happy person directs their thoughts. It sounds very simple, and I have been able to succeed at it to some degree. I am well aware of how tricky the mind can be, though. I keep working on this. And when I've had a hard time directing my thoughts, I am not too surprised to find that my actions at those times might not be too good either – meaning that they are not along the lines of love. When that happens, I think and do things that predictably end me up in some kind of pain or discomfort. At first, I was not really aware of this cause-and-effect process within my personal system. I was just aware of the effect part, the pain or lack of happiness part. This lack of awareness contributed toward opening little fountains of anger into my system. I am aware of it now, though, and becoming aware or conscious of the source of a problem is a good first step. The second step is learning how to uproot the problem. The third step is learning how not to grow that problem again!

I really believe that our lives are the result of our thoughts, and this makes me reflect on how I have thought and acted at times in my past. Thankfully, coming to grips with the process of growth has made me let go of guilt, because I've become aware that I am work in progress! Is this where humility and compassion sneaks into my system? I sure hope so! I am busily working on my thoughts and my actions all the time. It takes quite a bit of effort to be vigilant, but I know very well how it feels if I don't do it. The end result of vigilance feels too good for me to stop, so I am going to continue walking the talk! As the saying goes, *"The tasting of the pudding is in the eating of it."*

Am I happy yet? All I know is that the more I pay attention to the Golden Rule the happier I get. I would be a fool not to continue with this program. I share here some of the insights I've gained along the way, for those of you who are also on the road of Love, which leads us all to true happiness.

WE ARE LOVED

It is said that *"the wheel of God grinds slowly and efficiently."* This certainly seems true of the process of growth. Sometimes it can feel like I am going nowhere, fast! For example, it took me over 60 years to truly begin to realize that Love is the force behind all of creation. My heart keeps beating automatically and I keep breathing even when I am sleeping! I eat and my food gets digested with no thought or effort required on my part. If these life-sustaining facts don't demonstrate to me that I am loved, then I know I have quite a bit more struggling to do before I wake up to reality. Everything is in order – waiting for me to wake up and put myself in order, and then proceed to get myself out of the way.

Realizing that there is a learning curve to life has helped me get rid of the judgemental notion that "mistakes" are bad. This idea has been replaced by the encouraging concept of "continuous attempts at success." The first notion comes from a source of guilt and blame (which are junior associates of power and fear), while the latter has its source in unconditional love and peace.

The idea that Love allows me as many attempts at success as I need has led me to have a firm belief in reincarnation. There is so much to learn and enjoy on Earth that I know one lifetime provides nowhere near enough time to learn all the lessons to be learned and to become ready to be a co-worker with the source of creation. From everything I have come to know so far, that seems to be the whole purpose of human life.

It all begins with understanding that we are loved beyond all understanding. Then we share that love. Love is the name of the game.

HOW I FELL IN LOVE
WITH LIFE...AGAIN

I know for a fact that it is possible to fall in love with life again, or to fall in love with it for the first time if you've never done it before.

When a person is in love, they become more alive. There is a sort of glow or positive change that can be seen and felt around them. A study in the USA found that athletes even perform better when they are in love! Does it make a difference if they are in love with another person, with themselves, or with life?

Falling in love is a merging with the spirit of love. The human experience of falling in love is merely a microscopic, microcosmic version of the *real* falling in love, which is falling in love and in line with the Holy Spirit. That is the macrocosmic version of falling in love. When a person falls in love with life (the Holy Spirit), they develop a shining countenance – the sort of glow depicted in paintings as a halo around the heads of saints. Put in this context, the idea of nuns being married to the Holy Spirit is beginning to make some sense to me. I can, at present, only imagine how it will feel to fall completely in love with the Holy Spirit – I am sure the feeling is beyond description. I do, however, know what it to fall in love with life, which is a great first step.

For me, the process of falling in love with life again began at about the age of 62. I began to recall and get quick glimpses of how I felt before I started attending first grade. Back then, I often slipped into a feeling of what I can only describe as the utmost feeling of comfort – which was followed by an infusion of pure joy. It happened regardless of what was going on in my life at the time. I had a haunting sense of being in the scene of life, but not really of it. That feeling of detached beingness had made me feel vibrantly alive, which was quite different from how I was currently feeling at that time in my life. I guess this was because I was finding it almost impossible to find that comfort and joy in life at 62 years old, even in a part of the world where material plenty was supposed to make the combination of comfort and joy easily accessible.

I was quite comfortable with my physical experience. I was a healthy 62. I had a good job that paid well. I had all the physical resources I needed to cover up the inner discrepancy and lack of real joy in my life. What I mean is that I had enough activities in place to avoid having to feel and resolve the ever-increasing inner void within me. Now that I am able to look back at it with more detachment, I realize that the bigger the void grew, the more activities I sought or devised to fill it. For a long time, it was fun doing just that. It certainly seemed to be what everybody else was attempting to do, and I managed to do it better than most.

When I paused to honestly consider the state of my life, I felt uncomfortable. Of course, I realize now that life in a physical body is full of discomfort for a good reason: Souls are not encouraged to stay there. We are meant to realize the full scope of our beingness and spiritual potential!

I was no stranger to religion – my dear father was a minister of the Presbyterian church – and as I pondered my life during this time of inner turbulence, I was surprised to realize how deeply my inner core as a person had been shaped by what I had learned during my Christian upbringing as a child. I am going to mention here the main reminders that kept coming into my mind at that time, and will touch and expand on them as I go along:

1. Ask and you shall receive – in effect, you are never too big to ask for help.

2. Seek ye first the kingdom of God and everything else will be added unto you.
3. The Kingdom of God is within you.
4. Do unto others as you would like to be done to.
5. In my father's house there are many mansions, so there's room for everybody that God has deemed fit to create – Everybody is loved.

Perhaps you have also heard that we must become like little children before we can go to heaven. That is another biblical basic that remained in my consciousness and outlook on life.

I have also explored other religious faiths in my journey over the years, and have been shaped by some of the teachings and concepts I have come across. For instance, my core beliefs also include the ideas that:

1. Everybody acts as a teacher and a student. You can learn from everything and everybody.
2. Life is a learning curve and there is no such thing as a mistake. A wise person's life is one continuous mistake!
3. Do not judge, especially yourself.
4. There will come a time in your life when you must ask for a spiritual guide.
5. Watch your dreams. You can get help from your dreams.
6. We are made in the image of God, and we are put on earth to be shaped into the likeness of God.

I have also learned that we need to be in control of the ego. The ego is not an independent entity. It has the need to be accepted or not accepted. It functions only in the worlds of duality and only knows wins and losses – it doesn't know peace. There is no real happiness for the ego. In fact, the main obstacle between you and God is your self – the little self – the ego.

I've learned that Vanity keeps a person out of the arena of peace and joy, while Humility leads a person eventually to the world within. So yes, we want to seek first the kingdom of God which is within everybody, but it requires humility to get in there. Practicing the qualities of love every moment is what gradually brings a person into a happy state of being. What are those qualities? Love is patient, forgiving, nonjudgmental, respectful and honest, just to mention a few.

Armed with all these insights and understandings which I had gathered throughout my years, and inspired by the memories of my childhood, I set out to recover the joy I had as a child. What happened? Gradually, I found myself waking up from a deep slumber, falling back in love with life, and regaining a childlike sense of wonder.

This seems to be a journey we are all bound to take. Simplicity and joy often mark the first stage of our journey in life. Then, in the second stage, we develop ego, sophistication, seriousness, gratification…and discomfort! Stage three brings a return to simplicity again, this time with maturity and an infusion of more and more joy.

In stage one, a mountain is just a mountain. In stage two, a mountain is a complex composition of various components, which we play with and within which we hide. And in stage three, we return home like the prodigal son, and discover that a mountain is still just a mountain. The main difference between these levels of consciousness seems to be the different levels of joy and love.

TRANSFORMATION, GROWTH, AND THE EGO

I had a dream once in which some old geezer was making a comparison between the human growth and purification cycle and the caterpillar's transformation into a butterfly. The first stage of human growth was compared to the larva stage in the formation of a butterfly. This made a certain amount of sense to me at the time, and makes even more sense now that I am an old geezer myself. After all, there are cycles within cycles and, in this brief life of mine, I have been through at least three main cycles that I've noticed. In my larva stage, I was cared for and my primary teacher was my mother. Then my older siblings and my father and close relatives also chipped in to guide me, as is often the case. Modern living and civilization has brought variations and modifications to this early process in which we get a necessary taste of unconditional love, but the process seems to be fairly universal. It is even evident in most animals. Some primitive species in the animal kingdom may not follow this "initiation into love" approach, but most human beings tend to lean towards working with unconditional love when dealing with a newborn baby. I know, however, that it is also true that some babies are destined for an initial environment in which care and love may *not* be unconditional, and I speculate that this may contribute to shaping the character and personality of the individual. I feel that this is neither a good nor a bad thing, mainly because I am coming to understand that there is an underlying divine reason for absolutely everything. There are no accidents or coincidences. I believe the word "karma" attempts to explain this phenomenon.

The larva stage in my life probably went on until I was about 6 years old. Then I slowly started to learn the ways of the world that existed outside of my mother's protection. Slowly the environment took over and I unconsciously picked up survival skills. I started to harden up, for lack of a better expression. Perhaps this was like the formation of the hard chrysalis in the butterfly's transformation. I can only refer to it as the beginning of the formation of my ego— that necessary survival armour, which is provided by nature for a good purpose. Every sport has protective gear that has been carefully prepared and lovingly provided for the safety of each player. Since the whole world is supposed to be a stage designed for Souls to play and learn in, I think of the ego as the necessary protective gear for the sport of life.

Nature has set the stage for this play on earth. The trees grow and provide fruit for nourishment. We have food and playmates. Winning feels good and losing fees awful (which always reminds me of the expressions "sweet and sour" and "bittersweet"). At the larva stage of one's development, the idea and practice of playing has the illusion of being eternal. There are no worries. Interestingly, this worriless state is said to be the way we're supposed to feel when we come to the end of our training in a human body. Hence the idea that we must become as little children to enter the Kingdom of Heaven. At that point, though, we will also have gained maturity and responsibility, as well as the feeling of peace and tranquility that comes when one's personal will blends with divine will. When we are ready, we will be in the state of selflessness. We will be outside of ourselves, and the life force will draft us into the service of life. It is not up to us when we get "picked". This process is above our ego. Meanwhile, the ego has a job to do, which is to help us get ourselves ready – that's all.

PAYING ATTENTION TO COMMAND CENTRAL

A ttention, attention. Please keep quiet for a moment. I need your attention!

Close your eyes, take in a deep breath, listen to the sound of the air as you breathe it in and out. Listen to your heart beating.

"Be still and know that I am God!"

God speaks to us all, individually, and we need to pay attention or we will miss what is being said. Keeping still is the only way to get ready to hear this voice within. The mind must be empty – like the emptiness of space, like a chip of wood or a piece of stone. That's how we can come close to feeling some affinity with our true or original mind. The original or normal mind is empty. It has not picked up things along the way. It is like water that is calm, deep, and crystal clear, so that the moon of truth can reflect fully and perfectly upon it. Most of the time, people's minds are like murky water, constantly being churned by the waves of delusive thought. The truth of the moon still shines steadily upon its waters, but, because the water is in a constant state of turmoil, the reflection of the moon cannot be clearly seen. The result is meaningless lives, filled with frustration and misery. This is being lost in the illusion. So, we need to pay attention.

You can only hear the teacher if you pay attention to what is being said – by the teacher, not by the people around you.

It has been said that you are where your attention is. Any time

I think of *not* paying attention, I get this image of an astronaut who has landed on the moon and is not paying attention to Command Central because his (or her) attention is on something that interests him personally – yes, he has a personal agenda and he forgets he is on a mission! He is off and running. He will be off licking his chops for as long as his battery pack lasts. Only then will he be looking back to Command Central to be re-charged. Let us hope he is not too far to make it back or too lost to be able to hear and follow the instructions to lead him home. He might be too far to even see where the ship is! Cannot hear, cannot see, so it would be goodbye and good luck with that personal agenda, at least for that lifetime.

I have been there and done just that! I have definitely been lost and now that I have been found, I can assure you I won't even come close to doing that again! I do not quite remember the details of how I got lost or how I was found. All I know is that I was not given up on because I – like you – am a beloved child of God. Love was patient, and Love found me – and now I know better. I am with Love always, and Love is always with me! It took being lost to make me realize that I am here because of love, so now I readily and willingly drop my personal agenda and follow the way of love! I stay tuned into the divine command centre all the time now. That command centre hovers above and tells me where to point my battery charger to get charged, so that I can keep going and fulfill my part of the mission. I do not worry anymore. I just pay attention, listen, and do what the command centre of my heart guides me to do!

During the formation of my ego, I used to think of myself as a body with a Soul inside of it. I believed that my mind resided inside of my body too – just like my brain. I am not sure when this belief started to change, but I now realize that my thoughts and actions at that time stemmed from allowing my brain and body to act as the command centre. This is what I learned in the beginning of my formative years because it was what I saw everybody else doing, and school actively encouraged the use of one's brain as the ultimate means of survival in the playing fields of the animal kingdom.

Gradually, though, my mind and Soul have taken over as my command centre. Acting from the brain was good and fun while that period of my development lasted. However, acting from the mind under the direction of Soul is acting from the heart. There is a natural infusion of joy and happiness that comes when I'm able to operate from this new direction. By working from my heart, I'm also able to choose to be in touch with the source of life. This realization is one that I grew into gradually, and I must admit that it is quite a relief to be this way now, acting from the heart and directing the mind!

LOST AND FOUND IN THE PLAYPEN OF LIFE

The earth is really just one big playpen. No matter how lost you think you are, Love has you penned and you will be found. The gift of free will and getting lost is all part of the program. You see, the playpen is not really that big; it just looks big. It's an illusion. The huffing and puffing of our own ego and vanity is what makes it all appear to be so big. Take the hot air out of the ego and the illusion will fade away, and you will feel and do much better. You will be able to hear the small voice within and will know where to go. Stop looking too far ahead or too far behind, so you can see the obstacles right in front of you. Oh, and by the way, those obstacles are really stepping stones or stairs for you to climb up towards your destination. They are not there to trip and bruise you. That is not the way of Love!

Love will find all of us.

In the meantime, this lost state of being goes on for as many incarnations as it takes for the charge in your batteries to run dry. When we run out of options and there is nowhere else to turn to, our in-built instinct will lead us back to love and we will learn at last to pay attention to what matters most— and that is receiving and passing on love. Everything else will be added unto us, as the saying goes. It is that simple in the end. The childlike attitude is restored, illusion fades away, and real life is picked up again. There is no beginning and there is no end. We touch eternity. This is an experience that cannot be taught, though – it has to be walked. Again, the tasting of the pudding is in the eating of it. And the eating of the pudding is in the tasting of it.

SURRENDERING OUR THOUGHT BONDAGE

It is said that a wise man is one who has learned how to direct his thoughts. One thought follows another, without interruption, and if these thoughts are allowed to link up to form a chain, then you put yourself in bondage. And that, we all know, is an uncomfortable state of being. Thank God, the bondage is always temporary. Love is at work!

When we come to the point of giving up our personal agenda, we arrive at the point of true surrender. We become satisfied with a little. We wise up and perhaps realize that "he that increases his riches, increases his cares." A contented mind is a hidden treasure that Trouble doesn't find.

When we surrender, we also adopt the "I do not know" attitude. We are willing to learn and the hot air is released from the ego. Then we lose the constipated look that so many of us wear as we rush through the to-do list of our lives. We start to become transparent and can be filled with and reflect light. And, as we deflate the ego, we learn that the ones who do not try to possess "it" cannot lose "it"!

In the beginning of surrender we learn to go with the flow – and when we get good at that then we "flow with the go"! We learn to take charge. We become the trusted captain of our personal vehicle in Love's fleet of vehicles. When you totally surrender, you fear nothing, hope for nothing. You are free and, as Lao Tzu put it, *without even leaving your house, you will know the whole universe.*

So, child of God, wherever you are, just keep taking one step at a time. This is what is waiting for you. You will earn your visa to the state of happiness. Do not forget to ask for help whenever you know you need it. From personal experience, I have learned that help is always as close as my heartbeat. Help has always come, often in ways that I did not expect or understand. God really does operate in mysterious ways.

The trick to requesting and receiving help is humility. Humility helps remove the chain of vanity that keeps us in bondage. Have compassion towards yourself and humility will develop in you. I can personally promise this to anyone who is ready to take that step. Sometimes, though, a person needs to come to the end of their rope before the pain makes them cry out for help – and that is okay, too. It happened to me. We all reach the next level one step at a time. It took me some time to develop patience and enjoy taking the steps. Just by being yourself you will bring a personal rhythm into taking the steps in your life, and soon you too will be dancing up the stairs with a song in your heart! Then life is good.

OUTER AND INNER ORDER: STEPS TO KNOWING YOURSELF

You can become yourself only as you get to know yourself. However, I do not believe you can get to know yourself by thinking. I believe it can only be achieved by doing. By doing your duties you will know eventually (or maybe right away) what you amount to. What duties, you ask? Whatever the day calls for is your duty. Since charity begins at home, as they say, you first have to know and love and take care of yourself before you are ready and able to know and love anyone or anything else. This means that our path to knowing God begins with doing whatever the day calls for, one day at a time. The simplicity of life never ceases to amaze me.

When I started to pay attention to my daily duties, I became aware that most of the things I did were done with the wrong attitude, most of the time. Ultimately, I came to realize that if I start my day with an attitude of gratitude it is an effortless effort to get organized, because I am grateful to be alive. I am not taking life for granted. For me, this is the right attitude to take in doing all things, every day. When I hold this attitude as I do what needs to be done in my life, my heart stays open and I make the time and space to connect with love every day. Surrendering to the life force in this way has been very gradual and is becoming more enjoyable, and this makes living in gratitude a beautiful adventure.

When I set out to do my daily duties with this grateful attitude, I gained a deeper insight and appreciation for the importance of inner and outer order in our lives. For example, one day I felt the need to clean and tidy my apartment, since this duty had somehow been neglected due to other pressing tasks. I used to wonder why that kept happening! After all, I find a tidy and clean home very invigorating, so why do I ever allow my place to get messy? If I am going to embrace the next moment with the maximum energy available, then I need a basic structure or discipline to work with. Cleanliness and being tidy is a must for me, because having a clean home base helps centre me, and the order then spreads out to everything I am in touch with. Really, though, this order and cleanliness starts with being as pure in the heart as possible – and this spreads to the mind and then to the body.

The ancient Egyptians believed that the visa to the land of happiness was dependent on how clean or light a person's heart was. As I reflected on this, I figured that I must not be leading a balanced life, which in turn was not promoting a wholesome and happy life. I was not paying enough attention to some basic building blocks that create a solid foundation for happiness.

That brings us right back to charity beginning at home. It really does. To be filled with love, and to constantly think and act with love, seems to be the hardest task on earth. The person able to do this is probably referred to as an enlightened Soul. So how do the rest of us get there? Well, since love initially flows from the inside out, it helps when we're able to go inside ourselves and gain access to our source of life and love. Since our basic day-to-day duties involve things in the *outside* word, we must make sure that our outside affairs are in order so that we can successfully go *inside*, within ourselves, to turn the love on. Constant vigilance in our outside affairs (also known as 'discipline') therefore looms large in one's effort to successfully go within on a regular basis and get the love source flowing. When our outside duties are neglected, disorder ensues and there is a tendency to be "locked in" on the outside, away from the inner realm of our heart. We're distracted most of the time in this state, and chances are that our connection to the source of love will be neglected and dwindle away. Then, before we know it, unhappiness sneaks in. That's why keeping our outside affairs as simple as possible is a necessary step to happiness. Outer order supports inner order, which paves the way for greater experiences of love.

THE BULLY AND THE PLAY OF LOVE

Love is the strongest force in the universe. Becoming aware of this is the beginning of the end of thinking that we're victims of the bully. Is there always a bully? It seems like there is – this is probably the Law of the Jungle in action. The purpose of the bully is to make sure that every Soul eventually learns to focus on love (the heart) and graduates from the land of pain and sorrow. Yes, the bully has a job to do – for God. Is that not ironic? What takes us so long to realize that the Devil or Satan also depends on love for its existence? I believe that to be the biggest paradox in life. Once a person becomes aware of this, they can't help but relax and focus on working with love, which allows them to move towards personal freedom and happiness. Being able to focus is the way to move through the outside distractions.

So, there is always a bully – and there is always a guide. Maybe at times the bully and the guide can be one and the same source, or person, or entity. They are both there to help guide each Soul to their heart, the entrance to the arena of love which the source of life has lovingly placed within every human being.

Focusing on love began for me with the daily practice of gratitude. The whole experience of life changes dramatically for me every time I'm able to arrive at a deep state of gratitude. I mean gratitude for everything, even for the bully. It usually takes me a bit of time to get to the point where I can sincerely say, "Thank you for allowing me to be a part of this presentation here and now." It takes a little while for me to fully sink into the realization that the present moment is not all about me – because it will be here whether I am here or not. The presentation of life that is taking place here and now is actually a present, or a gift to me, because I am being given the opportunity to be a conscious part of it. It's not about me, but it is for me!

So, the feeling and expression of gratitude is like saying thank you both for a ticket to a movie or a play, and for being given the opportunity to play a part in that show. All I am required to do is to infuse as much love into every moment as possible, in every role that I find myself being allowed to play. For example, if I find myself in the role of talking to a neighbour, all I need to do is show as much respect as I can, not judge the neighbour in any way, and be honest about whatever we are talking about. I realize that each time I communicate with a neighbour could very well be the last presentation I get to participate in, so I do my best to keep any personal agendas of mine from interfering with that presentation of love. The more successful I am at this, the better I will enjoy and understand the whole show, and the happier I will be.

I'm not always able to get there. Plans, expectations, and desires often interfere with my depth of gratitude, but I know how it feels when I am successful. I also know that, just as I successfully learned how to walk, I will eventually also successfully learn how to work with love. Baby steps. That's what it takes, and there is always help available, whether I am aware of it or not. The help comes from the guide. Usually, though, the kind of help I need is not the kind of help I expect, so I am gradually learning to drop my expectations. I mean, really! I have been given the gift of a ticket to a show, and am permitted to consciously participate in the show, and I have the audacity to insert my personal agendas and expectations into the show? It's a wonder I am still allowed to continue!

The source of life has been extremely patient with me. Again, it is time to say thank you! I now know that the life force is always with me, and I am tired of not being conscious and aware of its presence more often than not. So, I have made the decision to take all the steps necessary to gain that exalted feeling of being conscious of it presence as often as is possible while in human form. This is something we can all do! I've heard and read that, as long as we have a body to take care of, it is not realistically possible to be conscious of this flow from the source *all* the time, but I am also wising up to the fact that there is always another step we can take in the learning curve of life. It actually *does* get better and better with practice, and I am getting better at achieving that feeling of happiness and joy and increase in awareness that comes when we work with love.

LEARNING TO DIE DAILY

There is an expression from the Christian Bible about 'dying daily', which I am still doing my best to understand. I think it has to do with letting go. I believe that if a person learns to empty the mind of all past happenings and all future expectations, then the present will have a better chance of presenting itself – with all the energy and freshness that it possesses. In other words, the person will have a better chance to experience the fresh energy that is always offered in the present moment.

I first learned of this idea or principle many years ago. I heard that dying daily was an integral part of an ever-expanding consciousness beyond the realms of temporal existence. However, at that time, it was only a mental concept for me. So, I hesitantly started to practice dying daily with my mind. Poor me, I was not aware then that the mental realm (and that includes the realm of my mind) is also part of the temporal world I was trying to transcend. So, every night before I went to sleep, I would think of the possibility of not waking up again. On the up side, this forced me to remember to make peace each day with every person I encountered (friends and foes alike) and, most importantly, with myself. Unknowingly, I had started the practice of forgiveness and humility, because forgiveness towards self is the introduction of humility of self.

Facing my mortality every day also gave me the opportunity to really be grateful for life when I got up in the morning. I had no idea at that time that having the courage to face my mortality was also the beginning of my adventures in the immortal worlds of Spirit. The idea that we are not our bodies but are indeed spiritual beings was very exciting to me, even as a mental concept, and now it is even more exciting as a conscious realization. My awareness of being active as a spiritual being has been like a small flame that keeps growing bigger, consuming more and more as it grows. This expansive feeling of freedom from the grips of mortality and the sense of gratitude for each day is waiting to be experienced by everyone who eventually begins to walk this path – when they are ready.

I have personally tried quite a few techniques in my exploration of this concept of dying daily. Every morning and night I make a conscious effort and do my best to empty my mind of all past and future events. I sit or lie down, breathe properly, try to be still, and chant various sounds. When I am successful, these sounds act like ice breakers that help me penetrate the solid barriers of my thoughts. It took practice over a long period of time, but I now do this on a regular basis, and I do not miss a session anymore. Sometimes all I need is five minutes, but going a day without this spiritual practice is like going a day without having a meal.

Eventually, there was a point where dying daily stopped being just a mental concept and instead became a reality for me. It is a pity that words cannot truly describe this incredible experience – but words are part of the mental realm, and trying to describe anything beyond the mind with words is just a futile effort – an exercise in frustration. I suppose that is why it is always said that a path to the world of spirit can only be walked, not taught. You can only know it by experiencing it for yourself.

The practice of learning to die daily has really helped me to be aware of how the ego, or the little self, can interfere with my effectiveness in participating in life. The ego is like a cloud that prevents the sun (Soul) from shining through. The process of dying daily helps to slowly dissolve the ego into the ocean of love and mercy which is the source of all life.

During the process of dying daily, a person actively rids themselves of guilt and blame as they practice forgiveness of others and themselves. This process also helps empty the mind of negative things picked up along the way in life. The mind slowly becomes like the so called "original mind" – the childlike, fresh mind that is more capable of seeing things as they really are. I've heard, for instance, that it is so much easier for immigrant children to learn a new language and pick up a new system than their parents, whose minds are "full of stuff". Likewise, it is easier to learn love when we set aside all the stuff and nonsense of the mind.

The Christian Bible says we must become like little children before we can enter Heaven. This hints to us that we must return to the "original mind" that we were supplied with, before we are allowed back home. A clear mind and a pure heart seem to be prerequisites. This necessary shift back to the original mind may be seen as an inevitable purification process. You simply can't resist it. I have heard it described as the irresistible magnetic pull of Soul, drawing us back to our true spiritual nature and home. I also hear that when God has hold of you, It will not let you go. Isn't that nice! It sounds like love. For me, it is a "waking up" process, like slowly coming awake, the cobwebs coming off the eyes. Again, I am going to repeat myself and state that I believe this will happen to everybody – like all babies are supposed to walk and talk, sooner or later. It is nature at work!

Heaven exists in everyone and everyone has access to it, through their heart. So maybe it is true, after all, that truth can only be caught and not taught. It has taken me over 60 years in life (and who knows how many incarnations) to catch this simple truth.

FROM DUALITY TO THE MIDDLE PATH

Tyranny of the mind is one of the ills that plagues man loudly and fiercely. It is well known that the mind is the ultimate double-edged sword. It can be a good servant or a very nasty master. A wise man is the one who has learned to direct or control the mind. A person who is not yet wise is mostly under the influence of the mind. And a mind which is not under the direction of Soul is unquestionably under the influence of the senses, and is therefore prey to all the ills of the ego.

In life on earth, which is the realm of duality, we are constantly under the influence of either the positive force or the negative force. To paraphrase Bob Dylan, you have to serve one or the other – God or the devil – you get to choose. I've often wondered if there is a third choice: Just be! Maybe there is. It's a thought. Maybe that is what the middle path is about! Just being yourself. Being in the world but not being of it.

"Be still and know that I am God. Be still and know that I am. Be still and know. Be still. Be."

Tranquility is the word used to describe the state of being beyond the tyranny of the mind, and it must be earned, not learned. It requires effort to earn the ability to operate beyond the world of duality. So, how does a person earn control over their own mind? I suppose by being in touch with their Spirit self, meaning who they are as Soul, as a spiritual being. And how do we accomplish that? I heard of and have learned something called spiritual exercises, practices that keep a person tuned to their Spirit self, just as physical exercises keep a person tuned to their physical body. I know there are also spiritual guides out there who successfully teach people how to effectively perform spiritual exercises. This is worth exploring for anyone who is ready to get out of the tyranny of the mind and experience tranquility.

Another disease that afflicts humanity is that of ignorance. Ignorance is the cause of a lot of pain and misery. For instance, we might experience the pain and misery of holding a grudge, or of finding it hard to practice forgiveness. Forgiveness can be hard if we have not yet learned that no one gets away with anything anyway. There is lots of time to pay for everything we have done wrong. Life is very patient and that is how we learn.

Basically, ignorance is the unawareness of the reality of the Golden Rule and the Law of Action and Reaction – which really is just being completely responsible for your thoughts and actions. Some call it karma. You reap what you sow. Of course, lots of people are quick to see when this rule is being broken by others, but forget that the rule still applies when it comes to themselves. However, being unaware of, ignoring, rationalizing or excusing our actions does not avoid the ills or pain that are the consequences for breaking the rule.

Being ignorant of the power of gratitude also helps keep a person in bondage, a state of being which is not exactly pleasant. Feeling sorry for oneself and being full of oneself are also cases of ignorance. Neither of them promotes cheerfulness and happiness – they both promote being ill at ease with life. Pain and pleasure, sweet and sour, wins and losses are all integral parts of the worlds of duality. As long as we are in possession of a human body, we remain immersed in the worlds of duality, where pain and pleasure are a part of the experience. It's the narrow way and no baggage is allowed on that road. Consciousness is then an escape from ignorance. Being conscious of and paying attention to the Golden Rule ensures fewer experiences of pain than if the rule is ignored. When the Golden Rule is observed constantly and becomes a way of life, a person spends as little time as needed participating in the worlds of duality.

Can we learn to love pain? Without the practice of gratitude, there seems to be a negative mindset that tries to embrace pain – I believe it is called masochism. This is an extreme pole of existence where a person rationalizes being an agent of pain because they are in constant pain. However, the practice of gratitude gives us a different perspective or viewpoint, and an infusion of joy which can put pain in its place. A good example of this for me was when I was involved in sports in my youth. The training required so that I could do my best and enjoy the sport was often quite painful, but when I became aware of the end result of the "pain" – which was "gain"—then gratitude set in. Gratitude always brings an infusion of joy, so the pain became an insignificant temporary aberration to put up with.

It was the regular practice of gratitude that introduced me to the middle path, which is neither for nor against, neither positive nor negative, but is beyond duality. The middle path leads a person to pay attention to the latent God qualities that are invested in each of us. From everything I have learned so far, these qualities are Freedom, Charity, and Wisdom.

THE GRATITUDE ATTITUDE

When I was a child, the only way I could temporarily make all the continuous chatter in my head go away was to sing a song. My song of choice when I was growing up was: *"Thank you for the food we eat, thank you for the friends we meet, thank you for the birds that sing, thank you, God, for everything!"* I would sing this simple song every day – especially when things were not going my way. I sang it every night before I went to bed. I loved that song primarily for the tune I learned to sing it in, but then, with time, I began to realize that it helped me keep my youthful joyfulness, even when things were not going too well.

Somehow, as I got older and got really involved and swallowed up by worldly activities, I stopped singing my song. I am not sure exactly when I let my song and favorite comforter slip away, but I am guessing now that it was probably around the age of puberty. As I got busy doing what most the population I was living amongst were doing, the continuous chatter in my head got more complicated, sometimes more exciting. I had exciting plans in my head all the time. Life was new and I looked forward to the next day, the next week, and so on. But somewhere down the line, the inner chatter, which was mostly positive, got infiltrated—slowly at first—by negative outlooks on the next day and the next week, which soon spread to pollute my outlook on the future. The time came when I realized that my inner sense of joy was gradually decreasing. The continuous chatter in my head had now become a real burden, so much so that it started to show on me – first on my face and eventually on my body.

In the meantime, I did my best to participate in life with as much joy and enthusiasm as I could muster, by putting more attention on instant gratification. I began to look for joy and happiness in temporal phenomena like the next good meal, the next weekend, vacations, new clothes, toys and gadgets, parties, etc. I suppose getting joy from creature comforts is part of life, and I suppose there is nothing wrong with being that way for the duration of a person's life. Now I realize this is what life in the "Power Grid" is all about – wins and losses – and if the wins outnumber the losses, you keep on trucking!

Eventually, though, the creature comforts also began to lose their impact, and the duration of joy and happiness I experienced from their acquisition grew shorter and shorter. Not only did the duration get shorter, the level of happiness I experienced also lessened. To top off my frustration, I began to suspect that every temporary happiness would be accompanied by a temporary bout of unhappiness – at least for me. I thought this phenomenon applied only to my life. For all I knew, it might not be the case for anyone else.

What this did to me, in effect, was to force me to look for other available ways to get back the joy and happiness I had experienced before. Deep down inside me, I knew it was possible to

get in touch with that state of being again. I didn't see too many adults exuding a state of joy and happiness, but I kept reading and hearing that it was feasible, or "do-able" as I called it.

Then a good friend of mine suggested that I take a close look at the practice of gratitude. He hinted that the path of gratitude would lead me to a spiritual guide, which for sure would lead me back to my source of happiness. I wondered for some time what this spiritual guide thing was all about. I was not about to go climb a mountain to visit some guru! It would be a while before I became aware that my own Soul was my spiritual guide, or at least it would lead me to such a guide if I needed help to get back in touch with my deepest, truest identity and nature.

In the meantime, I "woke up" to how helpful my little song had been earlier in my life and, after a bit of a struggle with my ego, I decided to try it again. The struggle with my ego was about how childlike and simple this technique was for the sophisticated person I now considered myself to be. Eventually, I just told my ego to go take a hike because I was fed up with the life of quiet desperation that hid beneath my sophisticated façade. I knew I had to make a move or something precious inside me would be forced to take a back seat, and I would end up joining all the miserable people who were waiting for me with open arms. Misery does like company! That is for sure.

So, I started singing my old song again, a lot! Unfortunately, my old song did nothing for me this time, and the more I tried, the more frustrated with life I became. What was I doing different this time? I searched for answers in books and seminars and workshops.

Then, in my mid fifties, a very dear friend of mine who was also in his fifties developed cancer and died within a year. To say that I was shaken right down to the core of my being is putting it mildly! There was a severe pain in my heart. I started to do a lot of soul searching and came to realize that, during my day-to-day survival of life, I had successfully built enough walls around me to actually close off my heart to life. Of course, I had only been protecting myself from the harsh outside world. Then this painful loss helped open my heart a little bit. A bit of light shone through the darkness and I realized just how far away I had pushed my love, my Soul.

I had heard the concept that every cloud has a silver lining, but this was the first time I had experienced the truth behind that saying. Everything really does happen for a (good) reason! Although it had not begun by my personal, my heart continued opening bit by bit, and I could now see things differently. An abundance of humility swept into my system— that can happen when you get to face your own mortality—and I guess I surrendered my personal will to the Divine will. And *that* is when I experienced the difference between being and living from the heart, as opposed to operating from the mind! I started singing my little song again and I know I will never stop.

The liberating feeling that true gratitude brings is magical! The more my heart keeps opening, the more attention I pay to living a life of love, rather than one of power. I have this joyful and peaceful feeling of life opening up to *me*!

As I said earlier, the wheel of God grinds slowly and effectively, so I am learning the art of "waiting properly" (also known as patience). Like a baby learning to walk, I put effort into every baby step and I know life is waiting patiently with open arms for me to get it right. Anxiety is slowly being replaced by a peace that certainly goes beyond my understanding. And I now know how it feels to exist from the heart! I wonder if this is what the great writer Shakespeare was pointing to when he wrote his famous "To be or not to be..." line. We all have choices: To be from the heart or not to be from the heart; to be yourself or not to be yourself; to be on your way home to the source of life or to delay the journey for just a while.

Do it now or do it later. We have a choice and free will. Patience is an aspect of love!

WHAT CAN THE PRACTICE OF GRATITUDE DO FOR ME?

Gratitude leads to a daily celebration of life. It is a form of worship that keeps our attention on the force of love. It allows us to live fully in the present and to touch the flow of life as it is – here and now. It brings awareness of the hand of God in one's personal life, and we become conscious of the spark of God within us.

The ultimate expression of gratitude is being grateful for the gift of live, for being allowed just to exist to all. These days, I am getting better at living in ultimate gratitude. I am only able to maintain that feeling for so long, but the older I get, the more often I'm able to get past the limitations I perceive in my life, and arrive at this grateful state— and the longer I am able to remain in that space.

In comes gratitude; out goes despair. No more lives of quiet desperation. Jealousy?! Envy?! Misery?! Gone. In their place, gratitude helps one achieve:

* Compassion for oneself
* Humility
* Opening the heart more and more
* The ability to practice the presence of the life force
* Constant vigilance against things that drain one's joy, and
* A capacity for receiving and giving love that keeps getting bigger.

The state of peace and joy this brings also puts me into the realization that the whole happening of life is not about me (ego is humbled), but it is for me to experience and enjoy like everybody else. All for one and one for all!

It's a very good place to start!

CATCHING THE LOVE TRAIN

We are born naked, then we cover ourselves with the protective husk of the ego. Then we forget who we are and think that the husk costume is us! Everybody is in this costume of rags, like children at Halloween. We pace up and down life in our costumes, like caged animals, until we find the gate to our freedom. Each of us has such a gate, beneath the husk, through his or her heart, which leads to their Soul – freedom and happiness!

The husk – the ego – is just a rough, undefined, and unpurified representation of an individual in the material part of creation. This husk is like a cocoon, out of which a purified version of an individual will emerge. This is what is commonly referred to as the higher self, and it is a real experience that is waiting for everyone! This is the handiwork of the source of life – and with the continuous practice of gratitude, self respect, self honesty and non-judgment, everybody will eventually open their heart and grow into understanding life, and thus into a joyful way of being.

Our job is simply to join the love force that flows back to the source of creation. The "love train" is always running. How do you know? Because you are alive! Your station is your heart. You do not have to climb any mountain or travel to any exotic hidden land. The force keeps flowing through our hearts. When the heart is wide open we become love – and we can then give love. A closed or constricted heart flutters and wastes away. Being selfish does the same thing to a person. We are not supposed to keep love; we can only have love when we learn how to allow it to flow through our hearts. Then it naturally carries us back to our source of life.

This reminds me of a song which goes: *"People get ready ~There's a train a-coming ~ Don't need no baggage ~You just get on board ~All you need is faith ~To hear the diesels humming ~Don't need no ticket ~You just thank the Lord."* There's that gratitude again. Gratitude, I believe, is the key to opening the heart and letting the love flow through us. Then spiritual exercises keep the heart opening to its full throttle – and vroom! Off we go! Personally, I have made sure that I always have a living spiritual master or guide who has had the experience of opening the heart and keeping the heart open. What do I look for? Cheerfulness, humility and simplicity. I find it hard to pay attention to anybody with a long face who exudes misery, but that is just my choice. To each their own.

Opening the heart also leads to the cleansing of the heart. I think it is important to know that an open or a clean heart is not just a mental concept. It is a feeling of ecstasy which is waiting for every person who is ready to go for it. When we fully embrace the fact that we are loved and have been given the gift of life, this brings gratitude to the forefront. Gratitude is the key that opens the door to the heart so divine love can flow in. I will speak for myself, anyway, and say that this is what it is doing for me.

DEFEATING MENTAL TERRORISM & THE BREATH HIJACKERS

I lay tossing in bed one night, having a fight with my sheets and blankets, and not particularly having fun. Finally, I realized what was going on. I was having a struggle with some nasty thoughts. I also realized that these thoughts were affecting the way I was breathing. So I said, Well, let's see what happens when I take over my own breathing – that is breathe properly, like a happy and contented baby does. Then I put my attention on my breathing. That's when I realized that there really was a fierce competition for my attention being waged between my nasty train of thoughts and my choice to breathe properly. When I realized this, I had a choice of where to put my attention. I decided to choose proper breathing, with the help of sounds that felt good to me (like the drawn-out sound of HUUUUUUU.)

It's true that you are where your attention is! Although the nasty thoughts put up quite a fight, with persistent attention on good breathing and the vibrations of sound, that train of thoughts eventually broke up, and the mental terrorism and breath hijacking were over. From that time on, I have been able to consciously control such mental terrorist attacks and attempts to hijack my breathing. It takes constant vigilance, though, because useless thoughts are a negative part of the world of duality. If I need to put my attention on my breathing in public or when I am with somebody, I just sing or chant my sound accomplices silently to myself. This silent sound practice also introduced me to a whole string of inner sounds that have always been there, waiting for me to dip into them. These inner sounds can open the door to inner guidance when I manage to get my mind back in line.

It is widely known that the mind is a good servant but a bad master. When the mind is under the control of what are known as the five passions (lust, anger, greed, vanity and attachment), it becomes a bad master of Soul. The mind switches to its lower mode – the selfish mode, the mode that makes bad choices most of the time. A bad choice is any choice that is not made from love, the kind of choice that leads Soul into the bondage of the world of pain and sorrow. Still, pain and sorrow are there to make Soul learn to be better, so they are not necessarily good or bad. They are just reminders! Pain and sorrow are there to remind Soul that the selfish world is not its true home.

The selfish world is the dualistic world of turmoil – pain, pleasure, wins, losses. It is a spiritual boot camp, the ultimate training ground for Souls. And, as hard as it may be to believe, boot camp is a necessary creation of the source of life, which is Love! Pain and sorrow will be the task masters in the boot camp to make sure that Souls spend the minimum amount of time in there getting polished up! The pressure in boot camp is designed to turn Soul from a lump of coal (darkness) into a shining piece of precious stone, a diamond full of light that sparkles (enlightenment).

First, though, a Soul needs to become aware and grateful for being in boot camp.

The constant practice of gratitude and proper breathing can make this period of polishing and purification more bearable, and even sometimes enjoyable. Enough polishing, then, will slowly but surely push Soul to switch to the selfless mode of the mind. The mind will then be mostly under the influence of the higher forces of love, and the choices made will be mostly good choices. It is said that "good" is just a longer version of "God", so most of the choices made by the mind in a selfless mode will lead Soul closer and closer to God, and away from the arena of pain and sorrow. In that selfless mode, the mind is then a good servant, and tranquility, joy and peace then become our operating companions in boot camp.

When our attention is mostly on making selfless choices, the inner sounds that are always there begin to engulf Soul like a beautiful orchestra – most of the time. The inner guidance that I mentioned can also be accessed when Soul begins to operate in this selfless mode. It comes in spurts of whispers and nudges to help Soul make choices that are in accord with being a conscious co-worker of the source of life. Soul then works mostly with the higher mind – as opposed to the lower mind used when we are in the selfish state. As long as Soul lives in boot camp, the lower mind will still need to be used at times. It too has its purpose and place. This means, by extension, that as long as Soul is in a body and needs to make choices for survival, Soul will be subjected to some pain and sorrow, but they will not dominate us, as they do when we are in the totally selfish mode. Pain and sorrow then become temporary turbulences – to be navigated without fear or anxiety.

Life is love, and when a person becomes aware of this, that person becomes more relaxed and more efficient in their life journey.

KARMA AND LIFE'S PARADOXES

Life is full of paradoxes: You have to give love to get love. Selflessness involves learning to love yourself. You must get inside yourself in order to get out of yourself. And last but not the least, what goes up must come down. I feel dizzy already. Then there is the saying that I came across from a Chinese spiritual master who said, "Only one who makes no attempt to possess it cannot lose it!"

What all these paradoxes seem to point out to me is that the Holy Spirit operates beyond the mind realm, and it may be a wise idea to just surrender or submit to It and let It guide you. Is this where the reality of inner guidance comes into play? I am still exploring that issue. Apparently, it is a person's responsibility to get ready, and then the Holy Spirit will pick us up when It sees that we are ready.

I know now that doing my spiritual exercises on a daily basis (and sometimes I feel the need to do them more than just once in the day) is surely opening my heart and increasing my capacity to receive and give love. I am learning to love my instrument (the human vessel) and take better care of it. As a result, everything and everyone around me gains. The more my heart opens, the easier it is for me to step inside of myself so I can get out of my limitations, arrive at selflessness, and be of better service to life. And the more I do that, the happier I feel. I've become more vigilant in the choices I make at every moment. Every thought and action brings me closer or farther from peace and joy.

In the selfish state of life, you are busily "locked in" to the outside world of materiality and your heart is closed off to the flow of love.

Then the paradoxical feeling of being "locked inside yourself" sets in. This is an uncomfortable, suffocating feeling of being cut off from the source of life, a depressing feeling which can bring misery and anger. However, happiness is always here now, waiting for whoever is ready, able and willing to tap into it. Again, this is a state of being that we earn.

When I was growing up, I came to view being happy as something that happened only when a person sowed the seeds for it. Somehow, I always associated happiness with good karma, and misery with bad karma. For my little brain, it was simple. You reap what you sow. If you sow nasty thoughts and actions then you reap a nasty future, and if you sow good thoughts and actions then you reap a pleasant future. And the future to me was any moment that followed the present. The next minute was as much part of the future as next year, and I saw the concept of karma simply as what a person had used their God-given creative powers to carve out for themselves in life. This still sounds pretty right to me.

Back then, in my early years, I also envisioned two heavens. The first heaven I saw as the one a person ended up creating with all their good deeds and thoughts. The second heaven— the real one— I saw as the one earned when a person was totally consumed by Spirit, a state of being that is way beyond thought and, also, beyond concepts like good and bad. I call it the area beyond pain and sorrow, the area where there is no death of anything. I know this is beyond my poor mind, and rightly so, because this heaven is not within the limitations of the human mind, nor is it limited to any group of people or any special kind of person. Egos do not go there, it's that simple.

So, as a kid, my concept of heaven was a place that a person creates for themselves with their own thoughts and actions whilst they are still in the process of being divinely individualized. That is, a state of being where a person dwells when they are alone with their thoughts while still existing in the worlds of duality (meaning alive in a body, asleep—dreaming or not— or dead in a body).

I've always looked at happiness as a "pleasant state of being" that was earned by consciously or unconsciously working with love. The other side of the coin is unhappiness or misery, which is an unpleasant state of being that is earned by consciously or unconsciously ignoring the Golden Rule. Every time we hurt any of God's creation by thought or action, we also hurt ourselves. We close off a window of light (or love), and if we do not learn soon enough, we end up in a dark corner with the miserable feeling of being cut off from the life source. Such a feeling can get so bad that a temporary disconnect or physical death may seem like a desirable option to some people. That's what is called suicide. But then I've heard that we'd just have to come back again in another life to get the lesson right.

So, karma and heaven and hell exist only in the dualistic world of good and bad, and each person is responsible for their personal state of beingness. Joy, though, I find to be an elixir that penetrates my system every so often, out of the blue. It's like "treats" given by the source of life, as if to remind me that It is still here with me. These shots of joy feel almost like an fresh influx from the land of pure spirit. Sadness, on the other hand, is the opposite of joy in this world of duality. It's like an influx of doom and mortality that comes in every so often to remind me that the land of sorrow is also here with me. Some time ago, I learned that the practice of gratitude always brought in some amount of joy. However, because I was used to life in the world of duality (pain/pleasure, wins/losses), I could not help but expect a foreboding sense of sadness to be lurking around the corner every time I experienced joy. With time, though, I have learned that joy actually comes from beyond the arena of pain and pleasure, so I now allow myself to fully experience such joy whenever it arrives, without fearing a later dose of sadness. And ever since I realized that the practice of gratitude opens the door for joy, I have adopted an attitude of gratitude, as an act of self love.

HEAVEN AND HELL

We carve out our own spaces in life. Do we carve out our futures? Our Heavens? And Hells? Why not? We are gifted with creative powers, aren't we?

In West Africa, there is a saying that if you want to know what death is like, watch sleep. When we sleep, I believe we take a trip to worlds of our own creation – and when we are awake we also live in the "essence" of our own creation also. I believe that heaven and hell are realities we create for ourselves within the worlds of duality or polarity. I don't believe there is any heaven or hell on the Soul level of existence. There is no male or female either. I believe the gift of creativity enables humans to actively carve out our own heaven and hell. When we drop the physical body (or die), we spend however much time is necessary in whatever place we have created through our desires, thoughts and actions, before returning to another physical life to continue our learning in Boot Camp. This happens until we finish off our de-materialization or purification process.

Nature has put the aging process in every incarnation to give us the opportunity to get tired of vanity and lust and anger, and to taste heaven while still in a human body. It cannot be done alone, though. That is why nature split into male and female, as a basic reminder. Basically, we require at least another human being to be able to pass love on, or to be able to open the door in the heart that leads to heaven. That is why selflessness is a basic requirement for really experiencing love. Hence, the paradox: the only way to have love is to pass it along. You can only have it if you give it – and you can't give it if you don't have it.

I remember an occasion when some young people asked me about my opinion on life after death. They wanted some concrete example. So, I suggested that if a person is a bully, they'll go to where there are bullies. They all laughed – all except one of them. I found out later that he was a bully – but he's changed his ways since then. So even if my concept is far fetched, it did take one bully out of the picture!

I like the story of the place where selfish people went after they were done with a life. There was a dinner table there, full of the tastiest and best foods available but each person was provided with a very long fork that was too long to feed themselves with. What a predicament! Now that could be hellish. They were all thin and starving because it did not occur to them to feed each other. If they did that, perhaps the same place might be heaven.

LIMITATIONS

A playpen is to keep a baby safe and secure, because they do not yet know how to do that for themselves. We do what we know, and when we know better, we do better. In life, there are always groups of people out there who think and act in limited ways only because they don't yet know any better. It is ridiculous, for instance, to hear about the phenomenon called ethnic cleansing! Every baby is allowed to think they are the "favourite" until they get old enough to be aware that their parents love all their siblings. God has no favourites. The thought of being better than others or being the chosen one is only a sign of deep seated insecurity – but this perspective is allowed to exist in the world. After all, we must grant everyone the freedom to hold their own state of consciousness, if we are to work most effectively with love. There is nothing wrong with that. There is nothing wrong with playpens either! For adults, we call them jails.

A person who is aware of the whole does not choose to identify with only a part of the whole. How can I be whole if I only identify with a part or parts of the whole? So, I am learning to be whole. How am I learning to be whole? Through constant practice, which is exactly how I learned to fragment myself from the whole in the first place. Limiting prejudices and opinions all took some time and constant practice to acquire – so I am learning to be patient with myself and with other people. The better I get at letting go and letting people be, the better I am able to give love, and the happier I get!

We have been blessed with free will and the power to choose.

When we become conscious of this God-given ability to choose and create our lives, it becomes easier to stop blaming others. Then we can take responsibility for carving out our own happiness. The moment that I became fully conscious that I was creating my own limitations, I started to take down the walls I had constructed. I also realized that Life had lovingly inserted a safety valve to make sure that I would only be able to dismantle my self-created limitations when I am ready, which is to say when I become responsible and disciplined enough— just like a baby is only let out of the confines of a playpen when it is responsible and disciplined enough. Growth in consciousness automatically takes away limitations. And just as limitations create suffocation and misery, growth in consciousness brings happiness and joy. I call this process "spiritual algebra"!

PEACE ON EARTH

C an there ever be peace on Earth? Will there ever be a time when there will be no predators?

I know for sure, through personal experience, that pockets of peace do exist, among a few families and friends. Even among families, though, peace doesn't necessarily come easily. Every time a bunch of people get together to attempt a pocket of peaceful living, one of the first things they do is arm themselves, not to protect their little society against wild animals, but to protect it against anticipated human enemies. That paints a picture of a not-so-peaceful future for the human race.

The possibility of all, or even the majority, of humans being able to behave on the soul level of existence is quite low, though I suppose it is possible. I have heard and read that everything we can imagine is possible. I must admit, though, that the concept of peace on earth is very hard for me to imagine—and I am glad that my imagination has its limitations, because peace on earth is one phenomenon that I would love to experience, if allowed!

For a start, the animals would have to stop eating each other. Then would come the hard part – humans would have to stop hating each other. The Christian Bible gives a sample of the possibility of animals getting along in the story of Noah's ark. All the animals got along during the entire time they were packed together in that little ark, so maybe it is possible for there to be peace among the animals.

Peace among humans? I can't imagine this phenomenon yet,

though it would easily be feasible if all Souls could harness their egos and work effectively and collectively with love. Maybe this phenomenon happens on other levels of existence. My personal little viewpoint at this moment is that Boot Camp is not designed for that.

I suppose Nature could phase out all predators – make them extinct like the dinosaurs, or maybe change the combination of genes in predators and make them drawn only to plants and herbs. What about sea animals? They can all feed on plankton like the little fishes do. What about food for people? We can all be vegetarians. Plants are okay to feed on because you can eat the leaf of a plant without having to kill the plant.

Wow, how about that? I just imagined a start to peace in the Boot Camp! So maybe one day it will be possible, although, without the challenges, I wonder where we'd learn all that we need to learn.

GRACEFUL LIVING

Life keeps going on. I am learning to infuse every thought and action with as much love as I can muster. I am almost at the point where even simple acts like brushing my teeth and clipping my nails are becoming grateful and enjoyable acts. Doing something for somebody else is even better. I never knew that serving life could bring so much joy. Even the simple act of walking tickles me these days. (Maybe this is a particularly big deal for me because I have had knee problems, on and off, all my life!) There is no thought or act that is mundane anymore. Boredom has all but faded out of my scope. I am slowly becoming like a child who is seeing the world for the first time. When I view life through the lens of my new attitude of gratitude, everything feels new, like I am experiencing it for the first time. Now I know what I was missing. I had read about it, attended talks about it, but until I started to put it into practice (and it took some sweet time for my ego to get out of the way), I did not know that such life experience was real.

I believe that graceful living is when a person is brave enough to walk with the Holy Spirit. Perhaps you have heard the expression "practicing the presence of the Master", where one acts as if they are always in the presence of a spiritual Master. I believe walking with the Holy Spirit is the same sort of idea. A person ends up living in grace. It leads to living in honesty, being transparent and light, not heavy! The cleansing agents of honesty, respect, non-judgment, and forgiveness become your constant companions. It is like driving a car through the rain and being able to put all the windshield wipers on – at the front, sides and back – for a smoother stress-free ride. Graceful living.

The more aware we are of what is truly going on, the more respect we practice. This holds true for honesty and non-judgment. These three qualities become part of the nature of the person who puts their attention on practicing them in every thought and action. That too is graceful living.

Living gracefully is living from the inside out. When your thoughts are clean and your heart is open, Soul shines through, and keeping your body and surroundings clean and tidy becomes almost automatic. If your thoughts are cluttered and your heart is closed off, you can put a lot of effort into your outer appearance, but you just end up projecting a warped or crooked image. Trying to go from the outside in puts a person ill at ease, and predisposes the person to some sort of disease. Graceful living, on the other hand, can help a person avoid a lot of diseases. It also helps a person age gracefully. In fact, it is probably the best anti-aging elixir available to the human system.

Until a person comes to live in grace, they live under the influences of the senses. Living in grace means you operate at the top of the survival scale, within the elements of cheerfulness, enthusiasm, creativity, and with some amount of serenity and detachment. In this state, a person can do many things which would otherwise be quite hard to accomplish. In contrast, when a person operates within the elements of anger, unhappiness, grief, and apathy, they are operating within the nature of the ego. That is why the ego finally steps aside when a person is ready to walk with the Holy Spirit. Apparently, there is a big cheer from the realm of the angels when this is accomplished by any person.

BUTTERFLIES, FLOWERS, FREQUENCIES, AND FRAGRANCES

I have come across many analogies made in people's attempts to describe the onset and growth or expansion of human consciousness. The one that remains as an image in my head is the comparison made to the formation of a butterfly. Butterflies have always fascinated me for many reasons. There seems to be a lack of "ego play" in the moment-to-moment, day-to-day activities of a butterfly. They seem to float around and serve nature by pollinating flowers to spread beauty and life. And I do not know of anyone who is afraid of butterflies.

Older mature human beings are supposed to be at the butterfly stage of their lives. People naturally slow down in old age, though only in body. In some early cultures, older people spent time visiting the invisible spiritual worlds that they had spent time creating with their thoughts and actions during their younger years and in previous lives. The real butterflies were wise people who made daily trips to the home of God, or the "uncreated" heaven. The standard belief was that younger people are automatically drawn to all things of the body, but that the older a person got, the more they were drawn to a combination of things of both the body and the mind. When the body got old and tired, then a person was automatically drawn to things of the mind and spirit. This is supposedly when the human butterfly would finally get the load in its wings squeezed out, and would begin the daily visits into the worlds of Spirit, as they rocked back and forth in their rocking chairs. Little children would gather at the feet of these "butterflies" and listen to stories about the far countries and inner worlds they visited. Then the young ones would dream about the day when they would qualify to become butterflies themselves. First the dream, then the reality.

A flower is another thing that seems to represent the presence of pure spirit in a physical form. Flowers are a sign of purity. They are so pure that we can even smell their fragrances. Flowers also spend some time in a "closed up" stage, before they are free to open up in bloom, and serve life in many ways. When I was a child, I thought I could see flowers and butterflies engaged in a dance of life. I still think I can see them dance now, whenever I'm able to get rid of all the unnecessary thoughts in my head.

Before I grew up and got my mind polluted with thoughts, I also remember quite well that I could not only feel the presence of people but I could also sense the fragrances of the "pure people," as I called those who were probably enlightened or close to it. There are always people around who are filled with love. I believe that is what an enlightened person is, and each one emits a certain fragrance. Every individual is supposed to have its own frequency or vibratory rate, deep down at the Soul level, and there is a certain fragrance associated with every frequency. So, every enlightened human possesses their own individual fragrance or aroma that comes from their Soul, or purified state of being. Their presence can be felt and sometimes even smelled.

Not all older people grow into the butterfly stage, of course, but it was generally believed that life offered that chance to everyone, again and again. Some people were even thought to be born almost ready to be butterflies because they had been very close to it when they died in their previous life. Some of the early so-called primitives had the concepts of reincarnation and continuous growth in consciousness deeply entrenched in their cultural consciousness. Today, though, it seems that all the distractions of modern day life have locked the average person's attention solely on what can be seen with the eyes, smelled with the nose, heard with the ears, and eaten or touched with the mouth and body. This puts us back to the consciousness of the beautiful beast, the mannequin, the slave.

Still, a lot more people seem to be ready to make shifts in consciousness, so there is always the possibility of life on earth becoming as nice and peaceful as it can potentially be. Boot camp will always be a school for Souls—the school of hard knocks, as I have heard it called—but that doesn't mean that it must always be harsh and primitive. Boot camp can be turned into a rather pleasant experience. Souls are capable of "civilizing" boot camp, just as they are capable of graduating from it. Astronomers now say that there is proof that the universe keeps on expanding. Jesus the Christ put it another way when he said, "In my father's mansion there are many rooms." Perhaps this means that more room is being created for "Soul graduates".

In the meantime, before a person grows into the butterfly state, there is the cocoon stage of the ego or personal agenda, where the individual is "locked up" inside a protective shell, a self-created cage where it feels isolated, uncomfortable and angry for a period of time. The butterfly stage signifies freedom from the ego or cocoon state, and marks the beginning of a continuous communication with creation outside of itself. In effect, the essence of life that is inside the butterfly is liberated and becomes free to be in communication with the essence of life that is always operating outside of its limited self. Since Spirit cannot be limited or contained in any form, such total freedom is therefore waiting for every spiritual being.

CRIES OF DESPERATION
TO THE FULL MOON

I have always looked at the sun and the moon as satellites for Souls on earth. This reminds me of a saying I once heard: "*On whose door does the moon not shine?*" Isn't it fortunate that no one tribe or special group of people is allowed exclusive access to the sun and the moon? I am sure some ignorant humans wish they had such power, like in the animated movie, *The Lorax*, where an evil dictator tries to control the air supply to the entire planet so that he can decide who gets any air! It's the ultimate power thought for some poor soul who fancies himself deprived of love!

Fortunately, we all have equal access to both our solar and lunar spheres. It is no wonder to me that some so-called primitive tribes paid attention not only to the moon and the sun, but also to as many stars and planets as they could see. Modern man, on the other hand, tends to put his full attention on gold and self-proclaimed beauty. This reminds me of yet another saying that "enough gold will snare most women and enough beauty will snare most men." There is a lot of that going on everywhere on earth, with both men and women pursuing superficial beauty and riches. It seems as negative as it can get, but it is allowed. So are the misery and unhappiness that result from this approach.

The sun is shining. I have an excellent position in society and a well-paying job, a big house, and the "ideal" family. I step out of my luxury car clad in an expensive designer suit on my way to a top-notch restaurant. I have a "chiseled" body that most women at least admire (and I hope desire) and I feel like hell inside. I am angry and frustrated – full of myself and filled with lust. I flash my bleached teeth in a practiced smile as I sit at a table and wait for my female escort for the evening to arrive. I order a sizable drink of whiskey, to choke down my inner frustration.

Recognize this story? From everything I have come across in my present life on the planet Earth, this is a description of being in hell. We howl our discontent to the moon or take our broken toy to our father and cry, 'Please fix it,' and our father says, 'If only you can let go of it, I will fix it for you in no time.'

I have read in quite a few books that the ego has a hidden sickness or disease which is the result of a combination of several afflictions, which include vanity, greed, and lust. I understand how hard it is to be at ease with life and with yourself if these three little demons are busy at play inside the house of your consciousness. Apparently, though, they have a job to do. They are there to make sure that a person will feel "ill" enough to eventually get to their knees and cry for help from their Creator. This is when you either lose consciousness or open your heart to love, or your Spirit self, so that love flows in to flush out the disease. The ego has this built-in self destruct system because it is supposed to be a temporary unit. There should be no hard feelings on this issue.

When the mind stops churning, the puzzle is very simple. Just be love. Just be yourself, because you are not only loved, you are love. Again, the simplicity of the riddle makes it very complicated for our poor limited minds – and that is how it is.

BURNING UP THE EGO

The source of all life is love. I am well over 60 years old now and this fact— that the source of all life is love— is now slowly taking over my whole system. I have paid mental tribute to this fact since I was in my youth because I grew up with the Bible, and my father and mother were both involved in the church, but now my heart has finally entered the game. I have always wondered what the difference is between knowing something in your head and knowing it in your heart. Is it necessary for the head to know before the heart takes over (as seemed to happen in my case), or can the heart know first before the head follows? Is this the old chicken and the egg question?

I am going to leave that to those who are born smart enough to figure that sort of thing out, because I am otherwise occupied with experiencing an event of the heart, a process that requires being childlike and being ready to learn with gratitude. The only way I can even come close to describing my full realization of love being the source of life is that it has been like watching coal slowly catch fire. It started in me like a little spot of light, and it is slowly and thankfully consuming me. It is surprising how good it feels to be slowly burning up in this way.

What is being burned up? I know it is my ego. I have mentally known for a while now that an integral part of the process of human growth is the transcendence of the ego – when a person is ready. Now I understand how the ego acts as a barrier between human nature and the force of love. I have played around with images of the ego being like a seed that must split open to allow the plant to come out and serve life.

My present viewpoint is that love allows the formation of the ego for the protection of Soul in the school of hard knocks, as I have sometimes heard life on Earth referred to. Why would Love put its children in such an environment? I personally have no problem understanding this because I spent some time playing competitive sports, and it didn't take long for me to realize that the uncomfortable and difficult training we had to endure was actually preparing me to perform at my best. It also gave me a better opportunity to enjoy the games I was training for.

From my current vantage point on life, I view the school of hard knocks, or boot camp as I prefer to call it, as what is sometimes referred to as tough love. It takes quite a lot of pressure to polish anything! It also takes quite a bit of pressure to transform coal into diamond. That is just how things work in the coarse world of matter. As I say, no need for hard feelings. The husk or the ego is like a hard seed that is planted in the earth and acts as temporary protection for Soul – until the real spark within shoots up in all its glory.

THE BUILDING BLOCKS OF EGO

Apparently, the makeup of an ego consists of five basic ingredients: anger, lust, vanity, greed, and undue attachment to materiality. These building blocks are called the five passions. They form the protective building blocks that keep us grounded in this world, so we get a chance to grow. There was a time when I viewed these passions as negative features that are bad for a person. Now I see them as part of Life's plan – a plan I am becoming more aware of, but which I do not worry about understanding. In my younger years, I always had a lot of questions: Why this? Why not that? Now, the practice of gratitude has led me to put my attention less on *why* and more on *how* life works. I suppose I have grown into a more childlike acceptance. So now I strive to work with Life's plan, as part of my own surrendering to the force of life, which I am conscious of as love. The process of surrendering is slowly removing my anxieties, and I can see and breathe easier as my anxieties become less and less.

Being able to see better, I realize that the opposites of these five passions are the building blocks for the refined person. They are the virtues of the kind of person everyone will end up being. It is almost like light needs to have darkness to realize that it is light. How else will it get to know itself? This is the way it works in art, as well. Sometimes, in a drawing, depicting the shadows can create or identify the subject you want to draw. Can this be the purpose of the negative qualities: vanity, greed, anger, lust, undue attachment. Can it be that Soul needs to experience these negative qualities to be able to properly identify the qualities of love? Is this why there is a need to experience the totality of the ego before Soul is ready to get rid of it? Perhaps the ego really is necessary to highlight the presence of Soul and of God. Can it be, then, that the so-called devil may be a necessary presence in the development of each personalized entity engaged in the Divine Play? This would mean that the darkness has a purpose.

Every time I put myself under a lot of pressure I keep wondering if this is nature's continuing attempt to turn me into a diamond! Is this not what happens when light saturates coal? And what is coal? The result of saturating wood with heat! This could explain the discomfort in boot camp! So, what is the message of love here? Relax, your loving parent is in the process of getting the diamond that you are to shine so you can see where you are going. Then you'll also be a source of light in this purposely darkened training ground which exists for Souls' purification.

ANGRY CRIES

Are we born angry? The first sound heard from a baby at birth is usually a cry, as if it has just been told, "Hey, welcome to boot camp in the arena of pain!" I guess Spirit doesn't particularly like to be restricted – period. And not only does Spirit find itself limited in a body, it is usually also in the smallest body in the vicinity, at the mercy of angrier Spirits in bigger bodies. I can certainly understand how any Spirit would find it suffocating to be encased in a body under these circumstances. It could be enough to make anyone a little angry. But I suppose the idea is to make sure that eternal happiness can never be found in a body, nor, for that matter, in any limited form of existence, which includes the mind form.

Does this mean that there is an inherent deep hunger inside everyone that will eventually drive them to do whatever it takes to get in touch with their Spirit self, or their real identity as Soul? My daughter once asked me why life in the body is sometimes so uncomfortable. It certainly looks like Life has taken steps to make sure that no one will really breathe easy until the final connection with Soul is made. I say thank God for that! This makes me feel better about all my loved ones and friends. We'll all get there eventually. I prefer to hold this view rather than think that we have been put on earth to either triumph or perish—a view which depicts the source of life as an uncaring, unloving force.

So, anger strikes me as a necessary part of the play of ego, in pursuit of its individual agenda. Anger is needed to fend off opponents in the play of power. The big will eat the small, and members of the small will be angry and work for revenge. The thrill of victory and the agony of defeat provide temporary incentives for the support and continuation of this spiritual schooling program. Likewise, victory and revenge play major roles in the excitement that keeps Boot Camp working.

For me, anger can be likened to fire. It can serve us well, but it can also harm and destroy if it gets out of control. Like a sharp knife, like a powerful gun – like any powerful tool. From the attitude of gratitude, I see anger as an available tool provided to us in Boot Camp, to help us carve our way through the jungle of hard knocks. Each person will eventually come to know for themselves how to properly use all the tools available for the stay on Earth.

A CLOSER LOOK AT LUST

The subject of lust is quite a tricky one, I find. Out of control lust seems to play quite a role in the day-to-day lives on Earth. I am sure there's something positive to say about lust, though (There *must* be a pony under all that manure, right!). For instance, how about the reality that it has very close ties to how human bodies are normally made. In vitro fertilization may threaten to remove this ace in the hole for lust. Still, lust is somehow linked with the creative energy in procreation. Sometimes it even tries to have a close association with love. For example, the sexual act, a basic form of lust which is primarily for reproduction in most species, is quite often glamourized as "making love" when described by the sophisticated human being. I don't often hear that term used in referring to primitive tribes, though.

A lot of nasty diseases have been closely associated with the sex act, though, so some folks can't help but see lust covered with filth and degeneracy a lot of the time. It is also well known and well documented that sex has the ability to reduce a human to the level of the beast. This is not to say that sex is bad, but too much of any good thing can tip it over into the realm of lust. When approached in a selfish way (which often seems to be the scenario), sex can lead to abuse, resentment, guilt, blame, anger, and a downward self destructive addiction. Yet when the sexual act is done in a selfless mode (which can be a very challenging state of being for many people to maintain), I understand it can open the door in the heart that leads to heaven. So then, I suppose that sex also falls into the category of a major "double-edged sword" and should be dealt with, with the utmost caution. Maybe this is the reason why some spiritual paths encourage abstinence or celibacy.

Lust also seems to work closely with power and creativity. Perhaps that is why so many people in positions of power have been hurt by this tool of lust. And lust often seems to go hand in hand, as well, with greed and undue attachment – two of the other mental afflictions of the ego that cause people a lot of trouble. It can affect our eating habits and sometimes even shows up in the way we dress and move our little selves, our shadows. I wonder if the word demon refers to the signs and symptoms of lust out of control – like alcoholism, drug addiction, and all the other addictions, which includes obesity through food addiction. I know that every move that clouds the consciousness surely leads to a denser overall feeling – which in turn leads to the uncomfortable suffocating feeling of being cut off from the eternal source, which in turn... I could go on and on until I land in the land of misery – but I am going to pause here rather than allow my imagination to take me down those scary zones!

Again, with the attitude of gratitude, I can see lust as another tool provided by the source of life in the school of hard knocks, which is to be used with responsibility and discipline. Otherwise, like all other powerful tools, it can cloud a person's vision, and delay the infusion of love into a person's system. Each move that delays our growth into love, or into light, affects all life in ways that we may not be aware of. On the slip side, every time I'm able to see beyond my personal agendas, and can think and act in a selfless manner, I taste the benefit of not doing or thinking things that cloud my consciousness.

MIRROR, MIRROR ON THE WALL

I find vanity to be another very sneaky passion. Everybody has at least a touch of that light called Soul burning inside of them, like the pilot light in a gas stove – always on, waiting to be of service. All we have to do is learn how to turn the silly thing on. When we do, our true nature is a pretty beautiful thing to behold! So we should think highly of ourselves. After all, we are Children of God.

Now let me make an attempt at demonizing vanity. The part of the ego that is not lit yet is the part that can't see clearly and keeps harming itself in the process. Puffing the little self up, both in mind and body, is surely a demonically ignorant side of vanity. Such puffing up always leads to some sort of deflating or even bursting if Love needs to reduce the pressure for you. Either way, vanity always brings discomfort.

Another major defect which vanity can bring on in a person is that sense of everything being about you. This is supposedly a stage of being that every person goes through as part of the schooling on earth. It is another limited, suffocating state which is set up to remind Soul that it is not yet at home. Pride can also cloud the air around a person and make it hard for us to see and hear properly.

Vanity has the tendency to keep the attention unduly fixated on physical and mental images, which can cause an imbalance in a person and interrupt the state of happiness. I am busy learning every day that any thought or action that shifts me farther from my source (Soul) detracts from my happiness. Pride can definitely contribute to misery, if it gets out of control. This fact always reminds me of what has been called the razor's edge – that fine line, the middle path, also known as balance! And when I think of balance, I can't help but think of focus of attention and discipline–which eventually lead us to responsibility.

GREED

The effects of out of control greed are evident everywhere on the planet. Territories have been run over and colonized, all backed by greed, which has sometimes been smartly packaged as the inevitable spread of civilization or religion. There is always some justification for out of control greed. When does greed get out of control? I suppose balance comes in here also. There is the joke about a seriously overweight chap who runs into a very skinny guy and comments, "Looking at you, man, one would think there is no food to eat!" to which the skinny chap replies, "Looking at you, one would suspect you ate all the food!"

Greed out of control can be the result of a basic insecurity. I have heard greed affectionately referred to as the side of the ego that has the need to hoard, in an attempt to protect and provide security, or what seems like security from the ego's very limited point of view. The feeling of being cut off or disconnected from the source can set off an automatic response of hoarding. Whatever the stimulus for hoarding is, I am sure it must be an unpleasant feeling. I have heard that there are people on earth now who are hoarding food and water in preparation for an apocalypse. Whatever drives someone to take such action is based on fear, so I can't see how it would be a nice feeling! I take my hat off to them, though, because at least they are working to take responsibility for their lives. Eventually, though, the time comes to stop worrying. This reminds me of a story I heard about a child in Canada who once proclaimed, "There is no chance of the world coming to an end today because it is already tomorrow in Australia!"

Love has no need to be greedy.

THE STRINGS OF ATTACHMENT

B eing grounded is generally considered a positive trait in a person, and a certain amount of attachment can keep us grounded in this world. I have always wondered if stability and balance have anything to do with this positive side of attachment. However, the final or the most efficient state of being in a human body is supposed to be a state of complete detachment. True detachment is said to be the beginning of feelings of eternal happiness, joy, calmness and freedom – the definition of "peace on earth"!

When I was a child I used to confuse ideas of attachment with images responsibility. I thought that the two somehow worked together. Putting images into words can be quite difficult most of the time. Now that I am all grown up, I still sometimes confuse those two images but now I know that I don't have to be attached to a situation in order to think or act responsibly. Attachment has a way of inducing unnecessary emotional and mental pain. In fact, vanity paired with attachment to an aging human body can bring on severe bouts of quiet desperation. A lot of attention on an aching, aging wrinkling body can create a bit of confusion and insecurity in the mind of a person who is still operating in the "it's all about me" state of being. That is not living gracefully. Such identification is a form of attachment as well as a form of limitation. This seems to be a necessary phenomenon of life on Earth for the ego.

The ego is only a shadow and it is at the mercy of light—whether it is aware of it or not – and since it is only a shadow, it is always attached to something. It has needs, plus a whole load of desires, which is what keeps it in bondage or slavery. Eventually, though, we all learn better than to get attached to or define ourselves with anything that is temporary.

THE PLAY OF THE EGO

Is there any truth to the suggestion that the ego is polarized? Why not? It is a vehicle for the stage on Earth. Does the ego operate in the sphere of positives and negatives? It sure looks like it. My personal experience is that my ego is always on a roller coaster ride. There is an intrinsically fun aspect of a roller coaster ride (as many kids might agree), but the reality is that sooner or later most people get enough of it. Nature even lovingly packages in a failsafe system called aging, which usually helps us get off the roller coaster ride as we get a little older and wiser—although every now and then a few old geezers may still be spotted on roller coaster ride of life with frustrated, painful looks on their faces.

During my own roller coaster ride, I came to understand a few things about my ego and its tendencies, which have helped me to stay alert to its games, trips and traps. For instance, my ego loves having opinions. Having an opinion about everything was an important part of developing my intellect. I must admit it was fun, too. In high school, I enjoyed being on the debate team. I found temporary security in forming an opinion, and aligning myself with all groups of like opinions. This always set the competitive juice coursing through my system. I used to see this unsettling feeling in my system as an "adrenaline rush". Today, though, I am seriously working on dropping all opinions because I know from experience that they just cloud my system and block the light (and I want to let the light in now!). Plus, I want to keep on growing in consciousness, and I got tired of holding on to my ever-changing opinions, which would change each time I embraced a greater truth. So why get attached to one's opinions at all?

The ego is also impressionable, and it likes to impress. Making an impression or leaving a mark is how life in the material world works. Statues and monuments act as reminders of this phenomenon.

The ego is either led or it leads – this is just how nature has arranged things in the boot camp, within the world of Polarity. Is this what is referred to as the power of the pyramid, or the pyramid of power? Geese even fly in this formation – a leader and its followers. There seem to be symbolic reminders of this necessary phenomenon everywhere. Pyramids have been built on Earth since the beginning of time. Even huts and tepees were made in the shape of a pyramid. And people seem to vie to be at the top of the pyramid, which requires and depends on someone being at the bottom. The ego is never independent. In fact, freedom and independence are not in the makeup of the ego, or the shadow self, the phantom.

The ego is an insecure entity. Deep down it is aware that its existence depends on light (like all shadows do) – but it behaves as if it must hide from light. And, of course, it does have to hide from light, because when light engulfs it or when there is no light, it finally disappears! So, all egos are temporary forms. And that's just how egos behave, without view of long term consequences, pursuing a personal agenda. Everyone for themselves. That's the ego's modus operandi. The ego in Boot Camp is like a pig in mud. There is nothing wrong with the mud; it is all part of creation. It is just a matter of time before a person gets tired of being the pig. There is no rush to get out of the gutter, though. Thankfully we have all eternity to work with.

An until we leave the mud behind, the ego has a job to do. It has to make sure that you earn your spiritual stripes. You can fake it until you feel it, but you can only feel it after you have earned it. This seems to be what an ego is built for. Use and discard.

LETTING GO

Why on earth does anybody have to let go? And what is it that is being held onto which necessitates letting go?

The ego (a product of the earth) is not capable of detaching itself from all things that the earth offers. That is why it is necessary to surrender the ego in order to live in a detached state of being while still in a human body. Some schools of thought believe that letting go is part of the plan of purification that is in store for everyone. But what is supposed to happen when a person is no longer attached to earthly happenings while they are still alive in a body? It can be said that the person would then be free to float off and experience things that are beyond the physical realm. Is this what out of the body experiences are about? Can this happen during sleep?

I have heard the sayings 'effortless effort' and 'going with the flow'. However, one can only go with the flow when they let go of whatever it is they are holding onto. Sometimes people hold on because they are too afraid to let go, or because they are too angry to forgive and let go, or because they are just not yet aware that it is in their best interest to *let go already*! Or maybe they are not yet awake enough to even see that they are holding on to something.

Eventually, holding on gets tiring. Getting tired of holding on is the failsafe mechanism that the loving source of life has inserted into the whole process of growth! Because Soul is endowed with free will and creativity, effort is required on the part of each individual to help in their own growth. After all, how can a person become a conscious co-worker with life if they are not conscious co-workers in their own growth? This is why responsibility and accountability are integral parts of the growth process.

Another built in failsafe reality is the fact that Spirit is not containable, so sooner or later every restriction must be let go of. So, growth is inevitable! Or is it? Maybe if growth does not happen then individuality is lost and the whole process goes back to ground zero! Nothing is lost (since Soul is indestructible) but nothing is gained either and life just waits for further attempts – reincarnations!?

Another way of looking at the growth process is that there is an inbuilt fringe benefit or reward for the effort we must invest in letting go, and that is freedom and happiness, topped by an infusion of joy and peace beyond the imagination. The other side of the coin is that misery and fear are the factors that eventually push a person to let go – and let God. Humans will sometimes use creativity to mask their misery. It is called being serious. I have heard it said, however, that seriousness is a sign of mediocrity. A long face cannot be a sign of dedication to the love force – it is a sign of pain and sorrow. Cheerfulness comes with putting one's attention on working with love, and letting go of fear and anger.

As life has arranged it, the longer a person holds onto the past, the more discomfort that person feels – until the pain is too much and that person is mercifully forced to make a move. The river is constantly flowing; those who are thirsty can always have a drink. Every day a fresh wave of liberation flows through life, taking with it the Souls who are ready to let go and move on to higher ground. When we are ready to let go, we make the effort to do what it takes to do just that.

Ultimately, letting go brings a lot of relief and makes life more joyful.

Every aspect of our lives is affected by the move to let go. This is a stage in the process of learning to work with love. I am discovering that the process also involves letting go of all my opinions and ideas of what I thought God was. It was as if I had to let go of God, in order to be able to work more efficiently with God. One thing I noticed (and still notice) is the consequent change in my breathing. When I drop all my prejudices and opinions, I breathe more fully than when I am full of myself. My thoughts are also more whole when I am breathing fully; taking in a deep breath always gets me into a more balanced state of mind and being. Whenever I remember, I watch how I am breathing.

Funnily enough, there have been times when I have forgotten to breathe properly because I was enjoying my temporary state of misery – for example when I was busy in my mind plotting some nefarious scenes of revenge against some persons who I believed had done me wrong.

Forgiveness is often hard to practice because of the sweetness of revenge – primarily to the mind. The chains of forgiveness almost always have a base in my mind – and that is where the release button always is for me. I understand now that I can taste total freedom if I can release everything I am holding on to. Easier said than done, but when you successfully practice forgiveness, you release a person from prison—and that person is yourself.

Letting go leads to liberation which leads eventually to freedom. When I became aware that all I had to do to liberate myself was to let go of all the things I was holding on to, I got busy letting go of them all. Why was I holding myself back? Because I was scared to let go and, also, I was familiar with where I was, even if it did not feel comfortable. I was holding on because I did not know any better. How did I get to know better? Through life's experiences I guess! I have had a lot of help. That is how love works.

Help has come in all sorts of ways. Everybody is a teacher as well as a student. I have seen people do the wrong things and suffer the consequences, and I have quietly thanked them for teaching me what not to do. I have also seen people do the right things, and quietly thanked and learned from them as well. The world is full of obvious things and when we are ready (or awake enough) we observe and learn.

Now, not a day goes by that I don' let go of something. It's like taking a shower every day because life deposits dirt on me every day. Taking a shower every day was an act that I found bothersome when I was a little kid still learning what was good for me. So was eating on a regular basis. In the beginning, I also found the practice of letting go every day to be bothersome and unnecessary, until I became aware of the benefits of doing it. I can guarantee that once you begin to do this and realize the benefits, you won't be able to help but continue. It becomes an integral part of learning to love yourself. You learn to stay awake, and stay away from thoughts and actions that interfere with your happiness and peace of mind, and you vigilantly do things and think thoughts that are good for you! It gets to be that simple. Keeping it simple is also a way to love yourself, or let love into your system. I have learned that letting love into my system is loving myself.

The whole process of growth seems to be about waking up to life – which is constantly softly whispering in our ears to wake up to our divine self.

GOD WILL GET YOU

One of my most favourite expressions when I was a child growing up in Ghana, West Africa, with a father who was a minister of the Presbyterian church, was "God will get you!" I was young and naive and innocent, and I truly held no grudges. I was never angry for long periods of time, and most of the time I was filled with joy. Happiness was my modus operandi during that period, and I really did believe that God eventually punished every wrong doer, so I did not worry about getting anybody back for whatever wrong I perceived they had done to me.

As I grew up and my ego swung into full gear, that belief slowly faded away and I conveniently modified that expression to "I hope God gets you before I do!" Things got really exciting when I sank fully into the sensory play of life and I had the need to pad up my ego. I built the castle of my identity with a moat surrounding it! By this time, my belief in a connectedness with all life had yielded to the cultural norm of pursuing personal agendas. Forgiveness was for the weak of mind and body, for those incapable of exacting revenge for themselves. Only losers believed in forgiveness. Each one for themselves and God for us all!

The play of polarity was in full swing, and the modus operandi were power, control, fear, and misery! You won or you lost. The compromising justification was that God (if there was a remote possibility of there being one) was depending on each person to take care of their own affairs. After all, wars are justified every day, and so is revenge. Plus, revenge has a sweet side to it – even the thought of it did bring me some devilish satisfaction.

It has been quite a struggle to let go of this phase of being, especially in my mind. It got to the point where I had to remember to ask for help. Humility had to sneak into the protective shell of my ego to soften it up, so that a bit of wisdom could seep into my awareness. A close look at my life then revealed to me the fact that I had never gotten away with anything bad I had ever done. The law of action and its equal and opposite reaction became clearer and clearer to me. You reap what you sow! What goes around comes around.

The truth is that I don't get away with anything. Nobody gets away with anything! I realized that the "sweetness" of imagining punishments for my wrongdoers was just a way of preventing happiness from entering my own system. I was cheating myself. Hurting others was actually a form of self-abuse! This sort of thing can lead to self-destruction if not stopped.

Humility really is compassion directed towards yourself. As I became aware of the fact that I shut off the flow of light into my own system every time I did something bad to another person (i.e., disobeyed the Golden Rule), I was then able to have compassion towards everybody who I thought had wronged me. Forgiveness comes easier for me now. Does that mean that I feel better about life now? You bet it does! I have a bigger capacity to give and receive love. I serve life better. I am more detached. I can taste happiness better! I am now aware that happiness is always here, now. It is up to me to do what it takes to taste it. The body and the mind do not last forever; everything that is born must die. Other things that make the body and mind happy, like good tasting food or having lots of money and power over other people, are also temporary, and every temporary happiness has a bad taste of sorrow waiting at the end when we realize that it offers only a fleeting distraction. There is no escape from that. Wisdom brings this awareness sooner or later to all, because we are all loved. So, we learn to let go and let God, we learn go forgive, and we learn to embrace true happiness.

At this point in my life I am back to my childlike nature and my old motto has been modified and dilute with compassion. "God will get you!" has become something more like "God have mercy on your Soul!" Yes, I have learned to put my attention on the Soul instead of that caricature called the ego. It is a choice I make now, because it brings peace into my life and puts me into a less polluted circle of beingness, one which is more wholesome and free.

Forgiveness is a part of letting go and letting the flow of life take you back to the source of love. I had to let go of my tribe, my race, my social position, and—most difficult of all—my gender, in my concept of myself. Though some people may not be aware of it yet (especially men), it is not easy to deal with the opposite gender just as Soul. When a person can do this, they are able to taste life in a way quite beyond their imagination – at a Soul level of existence. It is unbelievable, completely beyond the scope of polarity, and brings an incredible sense of peace.

I had to ask for help with this. My love for my daughter was a big help. Life had already provided me with a mother and a sister, but it took a little girl to finally help me flip the switch! There was a hut staring at me all along, while I was going around looking for shelter! How often have I missed the obvious in life? Lots of times! But then life is a learning curve, and patience is a virtue of love; we are allowed as many attempts as we need! There is no rush. This race is not for the swift. I came across an expression that I like: "the faster, the slower." I am still chewing on that one! In the meantime, I'll just have to exercise patience and "wait properly."

Apparently, we should keep paying attention to our everyday living and infuse every thought and action with as much practical unconditional love qualities as we can (honesty, respect, non-judgment, plus the practice of gratitude and forgiveness), and the Holy Spirit will choose us when we are ready! The one basic lesson for those of us who are not yet "perfect" is that first you learn to forgive yourself (compassion towards your ego, which brings humility) and then it will be easier to forgive others! Charity begins at home, and then spreads into every aspect of your life.

I do not know about perfection – why would I want to put a lid on growth? Sometimes I think the idea of being perfect is just a trap for the ego. I love this expression for a big ego – filled with the exuberance of its own verbosity! The picture I get is a bunch of cells miraculously put together to form a body – given a brain and a mind temporarily, and allowed to walk around on a celestial body suspended in space – and demanding some proof or a miracle before it believes in God! I think God has a great sense of humour! That sleeping collection of protoplasm will one day wake up to be aware that God has been with and within it all along.

ARE THERE MANY GODS?

" *Without the self, there is no problem.*" I ran across this expression some time ago when I was reading through a bunch of Zen Buddhist sayings that a friend had given me as a Christmas present. It made a bit of sense then, and it is making more sense now that I have been focusing my attention on putting into daily practice all that I have learned about letting go of everything that holds my spirit back from merging with the spirit of life. I choose not to limit my spirit by attaching my conception of myself to a position of power, a race, a country, or a gender. There's no way I'm going to limit my "arena of breath" to any of these nursery forms. All of these limited arenas of consciousness have a role to play in the growth of a person, like necessary security blankets at different stages of human beings' growth. As awareness grows, these security blankets or boundaries become suffocating and uncomfortable. It takes a lot of courage to rise above them and taste the air of freedom that exists beyond these limitations, but a person can see much more clearly when he or she is no longer filled and blinded by all the junk accumulated to build up the ego. All that junk is comprised of necessary temporary things that are needed to form the imitation or caricature self, the so called 'little self', which by nature is submerged in desires and so is uncomfortably attached to the physical realm – the realm of pain, sorrow and death.

What I have discovered is that the source of life has made guides available at every border, to help Souls who are ready to graduate from their previous limitations. There are obvious and tangible guides, and there are also a lot of not so obvious and invisible guides. And how do you find these guides? There is a saying that I keep coming across in my explorations of life, and it goes like this: "When the student is ready, the master appears." In other words, when the ego stops being full of itself, it learns to ask for help, and help is always close by.

Is it likely that every major boundary or level of limitation also has a ruler or a God of that realm? For example, is there a God for the source or level of human emotions? What about the level of human thoughts? There are schools of thought that believe so. Some even have names for all these different Gods, who apparently work in unison, just like a history teacher and a math teacher work together, or as a grade one teacher and a professor at a university do, in the broader scope of one's education – different teachers all working towards the same goal. In the development or purification of a person, the goal is that the individual will eventually become aware of its identity as a spark of God, or Soul.

Can this really be the reason for we've been created as human beings? I personally believe that becoming conscious or aware of the self as Soul is the beginning of truly living. Everything that happens before this self awareness as Soul is like living in the dark! The real joy and happiness (the eternal throb) only begin when we graduate from the turbulent stage in the darkness, where fear and uncertainty rule, and step into the awakened peaceful state where we are finally filled with light, and where we can see better and serve life better.

My little taste of Soul made me aware that every human being is invested with a conscious spark of love—a spark of the source of life or what is generally referred to as God. If it is true that everybody has a spark of God in them, then I can also imagine the potential of there being many Gods – or many arms of a single God—to help us in our journey home to our loving creator.

If there are many Gods then everybody will, in time, get to be aware of them and there is really no need for me to try to convince anyone of their existence. It is true that you cannot teach a child God; everyone must find out for themselves. This happens when they grow tired of looking for happiness in all the possible outside creations (and there are as many of those as can be imagined!). Maybe this is why reincarnation is an integral part of growth in human consciousness. It takes time!

I have sometimes wondered how many incarnations it might take, on average, for a Soul to finally "get it" or "get there". Personally, I never give up on anyone I love and I know Life has not given up on me, though I have made my fair share of blunders. I guess it is safe to say, then, that if the source of all creation is love, then every human gets as many attempts as it takes to "get it"! The beauty of the program is that we do not have to go anywhere to "get it" because "it" is always here and now, waiting for us to be aware of it, so *it* can get *us*! We do not have to worry about getting it; all we have to do is put our attention on infusing the qualities and aspects of love into our every thought and action. Then, whenever we are ready, it will lift us up! When the student is ready, the master appears.

TO BE ON GOD'S SIDE

One of the things that still puzzles me is hearing a victorious sports team thank God for the victory they just enjoyed, which implies that God was on their side and not on the side of the other team – at least on that particular occasion. I have also often heard people thank God for saving their lives after an accident, and I can't help but wonder if, somewhere inside themselves, they also blame God for the accident, or question why God allowed that accident to happen in the first place.

In a classroom, the teacher is on everybody's side. The students who graduate learn to be on the side of the teacher because they align their thoughts to the thoughts of the teacher on that particular subject. I do not know how long it took for me to grow into the awareness that God is similarly on the side of every living thing, but after I became conscious of this, I made the choice to try to be on the side of God, or love. This is when I started to put my attention on the virtues and qualities of love and to do my best to practice them every moment.

Every attempt showed me how much more work lay ahead – but each attempt aligned my thoughts and actions more closely with love, and every alignment with love made me a more joyful and happier person. So regardless of how much work I know I still have to do, the influx of peace, joy and happiness has brought a lot of enthusiasm into living life. I am over 68 years old, and I am more excited about life now than before.

So, as I say, I decided some time ago that no matter what happens to me, I am going to be on God's side! I believe that I came to this conclusion when the practice of gratitude became a way of life for me. That is when I consciously became a servant of life. My attitude changed from that of a miserable victim of life to that of a happy, willing participant in life. Such an attitude of gratitude really is the key for opening the door to happiness. It takes constant practice but I am willing to stick my neck out and proclaim that this is true! I am not the first person to say this, and I'm sure I will not be the last.

Another fringe benefit of the gratitude attitude is that it gradually infuses humility into a person's system, and this helps to soften up the ego towards surrendering and letting go of the chains that hold the Soul in bondage to the sensual powers. As we all know, there are five main sensory centers – taste, sight, hearing, smell, and touch. Above these five senses, though, there is a higher, liberating sense called the sense of humour. Laughter can be a source of liberation from the suffocating influences of the five senses which seem to work hand in hand with the five passions (lust, anger, greed, vanity, and undue attachment to materialism).

I have noticed personally that the first indication that I am not paying attention to working with love is the loss of my sense of humour. Any time that I am not able to laugh at myself, I know I am getting filled with the exuberance of my own verbosity! In other words, I am full of myself and not of light, and unaware that I have slipped deeply back into the sensual play (life in the mud). The loss of my sense of humour is a wake-up call for me to align myself with love again, and get back on the right side of the equation.

I remember being in a classroom once and waiting at the end of the class for everybody to leave so that I could clear something up with the teacher. As I sat there watching everybody leave, I realized that everybody's path to the door was different and tailor made to where they were sitting. No two paths were the same! That is when it dawned on me that there must be some truth to the saying that the path to God is different for everyone. From that time on, I stopped comparing myself to other people. This brought more calmness and efficiency into my life. I'm able to think more clearly and align myself more with the frequency or vibratory rates of the source of life which is love! I am also aware that the source of life dwells in the heart of every person – we don't need to go anywhere else to find it. It keeps flowing like an eternal river, giving life to all, including the sun, the moon and all that is. Including me and you.

Everybody wants God to be on their side. When we are ready, however, we choose to be on God's side for a change! Choosing to be on God's side leads us to the awareness that God has always been right by our side.

TUNING YOUR INSTRUMENT

I once had the opportunity to observe an orchestra practicing before a performance and was amazed to learn that each performer took the time to tune their instrument before every performance. It made me realize how important it is to tune or tune up a human body before putting it out to perform in society each day. We accomplish this by tuning in to the universal flow of life. After all, we eat at least once every day. The same goes for drinking and cleaning the body. So at least once each day, we need to take time to tune in and connect with the source of life. Sometimes I even find it necessary to do this tuning in more than once a day, but I've certainly learned the necessity of tuning into the universal flow of life on a regular basis.

Humans have long believed that we are affected by the movement of the moon. Now there is also a dawning awareness that we may be influenced by all planetary movements. There might be some truth to these ideas. Somehow, I believe the heavenly bodies are not up there just for our amazement and entertainment. However, we are even more affected by the universal flow of spirit that dictates the movements of all life. We need to tune into this universal flow of life to achieve a more efficient and wholesome way of life. This has been done by people down through the ages, by engaging in one sort of group worship or another.

Lately, individual regular tune ups are becoming common practice for me. For several years now I have tried different methods and have come up with a tailor-made approach. Basically, I use conscious breathing, coupled with various sounds, to break up my chain of thoughts and give myself an opportunity to tune into the universal flow of life. Even science has come to the realization that everything that exists has a certain vibration or frequency. That's why various sounds help us tune our bodies (which are our instruments) into the various frequencies that flow through the universe. Sometimes, though, it seems like everybody is walking around with little earphones on that are tuned into the frequency of their choice. I often wonder if a person's behaviour or character depends on the type of "station" they are tuned into. This goes on until we finally tune into the "music of the heavens". Then our whole being becomes this frequency and we move to this inner sound.

So then, why not make an effort to tune in somehow? Animals do this with various sounds. Maybe we can learn from them. All religious and spiritual groups have various sounds that they use, too, so I decided some time ago to try various sounds on a regular basis and see if and how they affected my life. I now know for sure that constant practice of this tuning in, with proper breathing and the use of sound, is an essential part of living efficiently and happily.

KEEPING IT SIMPLE

I have frequently heard or read that it is a good idea to keep things simple if we want happiness in our life. The more in tune we are with the flow of life, the simpler and happier our lives are. Sophistication only seems to breed stiffness, stuffiness, frustration, and misery. I live in the city and I see how people can't wait to escape to cottage country or the wilderness as often as they can, to get away from the stuffiness and stiffness of the complicated ways of city life. Perhaps then they can hear other simpler sounds than help calm their own vibrations.

It is not too hard to realize that a human's connection to the universe is through the air – so their easiest and fastest way to connect with any other object is also through the air or through sound. Personally, I have always been drawn to the sound of the wind, which is a natural movement of the air. It is a primal sound (like the ones that animals make, like the humming sound of bees) which can also be heard when air moves quickly – at least on Earth! (I have always wondered if the planets make the same sound when they rotate in space). After paying attention to the sound of the wind, it seems to me that the sounds of U and O come closest to this "primal" sound that I hear all over the place. As a matter of fact, the tuning forks that musicians use also make this primal sound of U-O! It is universal, not restricted to any part of the planet or any special group of people. So, I have been trying out this primal sound as my personal tuning fork, and I highly recommend it.

I am sure there are all kinds of sound combinations available that can help a person break through the solidified band or chain of thoughts that stops us from tuning into the life force which is always flowing through everything that is alive. The life force is always with every living thing (hence God is always with us), so I believe it is a good idea to put in the effort to be with It (or to 'be on God's side' as I put it before). I believe the Buddhists have a saying that laziness is what stops a person from making contact with the life force! A friend of mine said we should change the one-way street to a two-way street, between ourselves and God. It takes effort but it is worth it! I believe that the effort needed is like the initial effort necessary to get some machines started – like pulling the cord to start a gas-fueled lawn mower, or the twist it takes to start some small propeller driven airplanes. After the initial effort, there is "effortless effort" as the machine gets going.

The initial effort to be in tune with life is as simple as breathing properly, drinking enough water, eating properly, and exercising. Physical exercise helps to keep the little self out of the way. Perhaps it is the old Greek idea of a sound mind in a sound body. When the body is in good shape it is easier for the operator (Soul) to play its role in the orchestra and thus become a better student in the eternal play of divine music – the play of love, or the eternal play of God.

We also need to be vigilant about our thoughts and pay attention to the daily moment-to-moment disciplines in life (like working in line with the virtues of love), humility, and eventually learning to wait properly with patience as life unfolds.

This initial effort needs to be done every day— it takes daily and constant vigilance to maintain our stride and rhythm—but with gratitude, it can be a joyful undertaking. And the more in tune we are with the flow of life, the simpler and happier our lives become.

LOVED ONES

The concept of reincarnation makes the topic of loved ones a fascinating subject. Having had many incarnations surely means we've had more than one set of parents before and more than one set of siblings, of both genders. I believe that a Soul needs to experience life in the roles of both genders in order to be complete, and it also makes sense that a Soul needs to experience life in the roles of every race that they encounter and interact with, before it can earn the right to be a wholesome being. A person who is full of themselves and still in the infant ego stage of opinions may have the need to stop reading this exploration at this point, and that is okay, but I am going to gratefully take the liberty of being allowed to experience life in its totality, and pursue this exploration.

The very idea of a person of a different race or gender having been a loved one in the past can present some people with an obstacle that can be used as a stepping stone to catapult one's viewpoint into the Soul level or awareness – if that person is ready. On the other hand, it can act as a stumbling block and set one back into an infantile protective shell of opinions and vanity! Whichever direction it takes a person is okay, I guess. I believe there is no standing still in growth. We either move forward or we go backwards and are left behind, because the cosmic flow goes on regardless of our choices.

Being able to embrace every gender and race with love brings a person into alignment with the Creator and puts them "on God's side", because God loves all Its creation. It took me some time to become aware of this, and I am glad I am conscious of this now because this realization brought a wonderful breeze of freedom and calm into my life, which was not present before.

The flip side of this exploration is that the people who are in our family right now may go on to others lives, in bodies of another race or gender than we have known them to have. For instance, I mentally accepted my mother's freedom as Soul to be of no gender or race, and I wondered if it would be possible for me to recognize her essence if I encountered it (her) in a different physical body or on the spirit level. Since a definite special individuality exists in the creation of each human being, I am sure I will recognize that essence anytime, anywhere. I have seven brothers and one sister, and I know I can recognize each of them by their voice alone, if my mind is calm enough. Of course, my sister's voice stands out easily, but I know for sure that I would also recognize the essence of each of my brothers through the vibration of their voice. I know I can do that with my mother, my sister, and my daughter and every female I have been able to link up with on the Soul level of activity. And if I can do it in this life, why not in another?

I therefore no longer doubt that I shall always be in touch with every loved one. This is more than just a belief, it is a realization of truth, and the peace that this realization brings is beyond imagining! I mean, that peace is unbelievable! Of course, I do not expect anybody to believe me until they experience it personally. Just reading or hearing about it won't take you there. The beauty of growth is that we will all get to experience it for ourselves. But isn't it nice to know it's possible?

I AM THAT I AM

Up until we become aware of ourselves as Soul, I believe we are what we think we are. Are we not said to be a product of our thoughts? We have been endowed with free will and the power to create our own environments and lives. I suppose this means that we keep reinventing ourselves until we get to the point of realizing that we are actually an unlimited spiritual spark known as Soul. Maybe each person is also allowed to create their own God, or at least their own idea of what they think God to be. Wouldn't it be interesting to learn that we also end up carving out our own "beyond", as well? Why not? I have heard the spiritual sayings, "What is here is also beyond" and "As above, so below". So, it is not a big stretch to grasp that, until the time when we are existing in the realms beyond our minds, we do create our own hereafters, which are merely a reflection of the state of mind we hold in our daily lives. This would introduce responsibility and self-discipline into our lives, starting with how we keep our bodies and our homes, and encompassing everything that we do.

Again, charity begins at home. First, we learn to love ourselves, then we spread the love around, becoming co-workers with love or God. God is love, right? Is it that simple? I once read or heard from some source that *"the aspects of things that are most important for us are hidden because of their simplicity and familiarity."* So maybe it is that simple. We learn to love ourselves, and then to learn others.

Loving yourself is equivalent to letting light into your system, or filling yourself with light. You can only be a light unto others when you are lit. You can only help others to wake up when you are awake yourself.

THERE'S ALWAYS ANOTHER STEP

What happens after we realize ourselves as Soul? Do we still need spiritual guides?

Well, what happens when we are responsible and disciplined enough to leave home? Do we still need guides? Before you have earned the right to leave home, your parents or an older sibling or loved one will take you with them on trips outside the house, to show you the world and let you familiarize yourself with the things that were previously beyond your boundaries. The same process has been happening to me with my spiritual growth. Yet we still have much to learn when we head out on our own. There is always another step and there is always a guide.

Once I learned to keep my ego under control, I became aware that *"what saves man is to take a step. Then another step. It is always the same step, but you have to take it."* I have this in italics because I came across it in one of my continuous readings, though I don't know exactly where. It is true though that we never stop growing in consciousness. Perfectionism is just a false goal. It is part of the ego! I also believe that we either move forward or move backward (and are left behind), so I choose to continue taking steps and moving ahead. There is always an effort required to take one's steps, but once you catch your stride and establish your rhythm, it becomes an effortless effort – that is what happens when you have learned to be yourself.

Becoming yourself involves being able to see yourself clearly, but *"it is as hard to see oneself as it is to look backwards without turning around"*, as the saying goes. It is almost like you have to be selfless before you can see and be yourself. Another paradox. But essentially, this just means that you have to go beyond your imitation self (your ego) before you can see and be your authentic self. The imitation self says, "Another day, another dollar," while the authentic self says, "Another day, another step towards God!" The beauty of getting the ego or imitation self out of the way is that when you do, all other limitations also get out of the way! You move out of the world of illusion.

ANTI-AGING

We cry when we are born, and the people around us cheer. The people around us cry when we die, although we are free, with just our bodies lying there in the casket looking all peaceful. It is the cycle of life and death puts the average person ill at ease. It haunts a person until such time as the trials and tribulations of life have made them humble enough to practice gratitude and get in touch with their deepest, truest, most secret and sacred identity as Soul. There is no escaping this. It will stare you in the face, incarnation after incarnation, until you do something about it.

In the meantime, life in a body can be amusing. I always find it fun to watch children play. They move their bodies in ways that would put an adult in the emergency department of a hospital. Yet all a child wants to do is to grow up into adulthood. Adults are good at projecting the image of having it all together, but it's all part of the Big Illusion. While children are in an intense learning phase of life, so many adults seem to stop growing, stop having adventures, stop truly living. They miss the very secret to eternal youth: You are only old when you stop growing!

There are quite a few anti-aging remedies out there. So far, though, I have yet to come across anything that touches upon the reality that the only thing that does not age is our spirit or soul. Maybe the best anti-aging process comes from inside of us! I am sure that when we get in touch with our childlike self we will know how to age gracefully. The Christian Bible quotes *"You have to be like little children before you can get into heaven.*" Another saying is that "*childlikeness has to be restored with long years of training in the art of self-forgetfulness.*" Only then can we taste eternal happiness. I have seen a few people out there who have let go of their vanity (a big part of the illusory imitation self or ego) and they can't help but exude their beautiful authentic selves. They look more beautiful than any movie star or picture-perfect mannequin.

Personally, I believe the only anti-aging process worth considering is this art of self-forgetfulness – allowing the authentic self to show up! I believe real beauty comes from within and not from the outside. Plastic surgery has a place in life but I don't think it can ever be an anti-aging solution. Learning to be yourself is the best anti-aging remedy there is. These days, the only time I don't look good are the times when I am not being my authentic self. Am I bothered by getting older? Not anymore! I can't wait to see how much better it can get!

EXPECTATIONS AND SECURITY

Learning to live without expectations has been a very difficult transition in my life. I used to base my enthusiasm for life on expectations. For example, I would have a good week because I had planned a weekend filled with some sort of self-indulgent fun. On the flip side, I would also experience disappointment when my enthusiasm and happiness depended on some phenomenon that did not come to pass. The only times I thoroughly enjoyed things was when I was able to approach them without any expectations. I am still working on this aspect of my attitude.

I remember an incident when I was a teenager, which made a very strong impression on me. I was home on vacation from boarding school and everything was moving along quite nicely. Then I received a letter from a friend in another town, saying that he was coming for a visit the next day. At that time, houses in Africa were not equipped with phones, so communication was done mostly through the post office, so this was the only way for him to let me know he was coming.

The next morning, I got up early and waited patiently throughout the day for my friend's arrival. It did not happen. The next few days were spent in anticipation, waiting and expecting my friend to arrive and imagining all the good times we were going to have, but still he did not arrive. It was torture! Finally, after a whole week had gone by, I received another letter from him saying that there had been a family calamity, so he was not going to be able to come. As soon as I knew he was not coming, the torture stopped because I dropped my expectations. From then on, I always tried to keep my state of mind intact, regardless of what might lay ahead. This is especially important now that I am aware that my state of mind affects everything I am in touch with – starting with myself!

"Nothing is secure but life, transition, the energizing spirit.

People wish to be settled, but only so far as they are unsettled is there any hope for them."

I forget where I came across this saying but it has helped me work to drop my expectations, get in touch with my childlike spirit, and allow curiosity to replace expectations. Disappointments fade away when childlike curiosity comes in to play.

TRUE WEALTH

I used to look forward to what the day held for me—like, another day another dollar. It took me quite a while to become aware that dollars do not bring eternal happiness. I was always hoping to be the first one to prove that truth wrong! I knew the Christian Bible stated that it would be easier for a camel to pass through the eye of a needle than for a rich man to enter heaven, but, as I said, I was doing my best to prove the Bible wrong. And I'm sure there are lots of poor people out there who would just love the opportunity to prove the Bible right!

We can only know a thing for sure through personal experience, and I figure we have as many incarnations as we need to explore that issue. So, I say, good luck with that to those Souls who have not yet figured it out. I find that a greater awareness brings a greater ability and willingness to let everything and everybody be and learn at their own pace.

Can a person become rich at the expense of another of God's children and still be close to God? I've never seen or heard of a person like that – but I haven't seen or heard of everything yet. Now that I have tasted real happiness, though, my own motto has changed. Now it is, "Another day, another step closer to God," because that is where eternal happiness can really be found. That's where the real joy and riches are.

ADDICTED TO SOUL!

When I was younger, I was excited about all the temporal things that life could give me – the foods, toys, physical, emotional and mental achievements, etc. Somewhere along the way, though, they all lost their hold on me. I am no longer addicted to them. I love them all but they do not have a hold on my heart anymore. I am aware that I am working towards being able to live in a detached state of being.

I had a dream once that stuck with me and changed the course of my life. I was in a darkened enclosure with a lot of other people – at least it felt like people. It was noisy and not the most comfortable place to be. I saw a candle somewhere in the distance and so naturally I made my way towards it because it was dark and I wanted to see what was going on, plus I was getting tired of bumping into things and people. As I got closer, I noticed other candles around me – but none of them were lit. So, I thought, good, I'll just grab a candle and light it and take it with me, that should help me see my way around and maybe find a way out of this dark place filled with bumps and confusion.

As I got closer, I realized that I was also a candle. It then dawned on me that the only way to have a lit candle was to light myself up. That is when I realized why the other candles were not in a hurry to be lit. It took burning off the tip of the candle to expose the "lightable" part of the candle – the wick. The part that needed to be burned off before the candle could be lit was the part that I had been using to feel and protect myself in the darkness all along, so there was a bit of a hesitation to go closer to the lit candle, even though I had an instinctual urge to be lit. There seemed to be a line past which, if you crossed it, the "burning off" would automatically start and you couldn't turn back or stop it; so, there were quite a lot of unlit candles in a state of hesitation, questioning "Shall I go or shall I stay?"

Quite some time passed before the urge to be lit overcame my attachment to my protective tip of wax, so I crossed the line. Actually, I think it was a combination of choosing to cross the line and being pushed across by other candles that were drawn to the light.

It was only after the burning off started that I got to see a whole other world of light and lit candles that I had not been able to see before, when I was all covered up! Then the fear of being "burnt off" turned to the relief of casting off the unneeded sheath. Freedom!

This is when my addiction to Soul began. There were years when my Soul was in my body and I had a lot of questions. Now my body is in my Soul and I am living out the answers. My body was in a cocoon of my ego, and now my body has the wings of Soul like a butterfly. I have not yet come across a butterfly with a big ego. They just fly around and serve life.

After the candle gets lit, there comes another realization that the entire wax part of oneself will inevitably melt away some day – this is referred to as death of the physical body. Next came the realization that the wick was connected to an eternal source through my heart, which means I am actually an eternal flame – Soul – a particle of the main flame which is the essence of God. I like the way that sounds – that's all! I love my new addiction. The way I see it, whether we are aware of it or not, we are always addicted and attached to something. Eventually the final inevitable addiction is to the spirit of life itself, through the addiction to each individual's Soul. Addiction then becomes a good thing!

Love is the final cure for every temporary addiction out there. Most parents love their children so much that they will take every precaution and do everything within their power to make sure that their children are happy. Since parents' love for their children is just a miniature replica of the love that God has for all Its children, I believe that the source of life has created every "help" possible to make sure that all Its children end up in joy and happiness. This is also, most importantly, why everyone has an intrinsic desire for God – or happiness.

With the realization that everlasting freedom and happiness rests only in Soul – and not in the body, mind or emotions – it becomes easier to comprehend the fact that life will make sure there is no eternal happiness or freedom to be found in any thing that is temporary! The feeling of ecstasy that comes when the connection to Soul is made puts to shame any kind of temporary escape or imitation freedom that any drug, power gain, or fame can provide.

LIGHTS IN THE BOOTCAMP

There are lots of schools of thought which regard the Earth as a classroom or a training ground for Soul. My brief time in the cadet corps when I was in high school in West Africa leads me to refer to life on Earth as Boot Camp. I was glad I went to Boot Camp. It was not entirely pleasant, but there came a time when I became aware of the purpose of the experience – and then it was even fun! In Boot Camp, help and discipline were strategically placed everywhere. I am slowly waking up and becoming conscious or aware of the reality that there is also "help" available everywhere on Earth.

I believe Life has strategically placed sources of light in the dark arena of purification or training grounds for Souls in which we reside. We do not have to travel high up any mountain or to some far aware "exotic" place to be able to get in touch with our Soul. In our ignorance, we appoint a few spots as exotic and sacred, but the truth is that every spot is sacred. If it is true that everybody has the spark of God in them, then it is also true that wherever you are, God is there too!

As long as I am aware that I am alive, I know that God is with me. Awareness or consciousness is then the only thing worth considering, and complete awareness (wakefulness) begins in the heart. From everything I have read and heard so far, this is what Boot Camp is all about. It takes light going into the dark to realize itself as light. Likewise, a spark of God must go through the Boot Camp to become aware that it is a spark of God. When we finally "get it" then we are ready to fully participate in life.

Is it possible to be grateful while you are being bumped around in the dark? Of course, it is! The daily practice of gratitude leads a person to the awareness that they have been accepted into the human being training program (or boot camp). Then experience will lead them to acquire the aspect of love called patience – so they can wait properly whilst in the program.

Again, how long does it take before we get it? Thankfully, we have as long as we need—life after life. The fruit drops when it is ripe. That's it! It is that simple. Realizing one's own essence as a spark of God is the ultimate expression of enlightenment. Enlightenment (becoming conscious of yourself as Soul or a spark of God) makes one a powerful being in the universe. Usually no one else notices, but that is okay because it has nothing to do with being famous or adored.

ARE WE ALL CONNECTED?

The encounter with my Soul left me with a feeling of connection with all of creation. The hardest part of this awareness was the realization that I had a connection to people who I considered to be some of the most despicable humans the Creator had ever allowed to exist. I had to drop all my opinions and judgmental attitudes to fully grasp this new consciousness of total connectedness with life. I had to respect *all* the Creator's handiwork – starting with myself, because I too am the Creator's handwork, a work in progress. That meant I had to be honest with myself and direct quite a bit of compassion to myself, which led to the infusion of humility I have mentioned, which in turn helped me put my ego on the shelf so that I could have a better understanding of being connected to all life.

I started to see life from a different perspective than the personal agenda level, because our connection to all life exists on the Soul level of existence. It takes quite a bit of effort to attain the Soul perspective, but I now feel as though that viewpoint is gradually swallowing or engulfing my entire being – and I must admit, I like it! The feeling of calmness that flows from the viewpoint of Soul is so attractive that, once it is experienced, there is an innate urge to continue experiencing it. Now, at 68 years of age (this time around), I am thrilled to finally know for sure that the Holy Spirit is taking over my life, and because of this I do not worry about what the future holds for me because I now understand that it is not about me, but it sure is *for* me. My life is occurring in order to allow me to be a conscious participator with love, no matter what it brings.

The feeling of being a conscious co-worker with love is beyond anything I ever imagined. Also, embracing all life is not as difficult as I thought it would be. Still, dropping my judgmental attitude did not come easy. It meant letting go of all my opinions about everything. So, just as I eat, drink, and breathe on a regular basis, I also practice gratitude, surrender, and letting go on a regular basis. It is a way of life for me now. I shall give up eating and drinking before I even think of giving up breathing and the practices of gratitude, surrender and letting go. I am aware of what my primary connection to the universe is, and will not let *it* go!

My own process of letting go and letting God has resulted in the emergence of a childlike quality in my attitude towards life. I have regained a trust and curiosity that I had almost lost. It is not a trust in people; it is more a trust in the source of life. Every day, everything and every event has a fresh feeling about it! I have lost that popular apathetic "same old, same old" approach to life. Everything seems to be changing every day. It has taken me some time to adjust to this new, ever-changing but peaceful feeling. It's almost like watching a movie and being a part of it at the same time, with the choice to improve in my role at any time. I suppose this is just a small sample of living in a detached state.

I look forward to the next moment with the same childlike fresh attitude. The enthusiasm is not about what I can personally gain from life. It is more about how much better I can serve life in every situation I am presented with. Life really begins when it stops being "about you". It seems that old age comes with the fringe benefit of potentially making it easier to forgo the sensual play of the ego, so that one can really taste life. It is painful to watch an old person with a big ego who is still chained down by the five passions of lust, anger, vanity, greed, and undue attachment to material things. It is almost pathetic and embarrassing to watch, like seeing an untrained dog lead its owner into trouble. The ego is supposed to end up like a well-trained guard dog or service dog to Soul, not the other way around! True happiness begins only when your dog (your ego) is under control. Until that time, there is persistent turbulence and uncertainty.

Becoming aware of my connection with all life also makes me pay more attention to my thoughts and actions. I am more aware now that every bad thought or action against another human being just leads to shutting out more light and happiness from my own system. I realize, too, that true happiness means being able to embrace and breathe in the whole thing—being wholesome— and not just grabbing a part of the whole and disappearing into a hole with it like a scared animal. Fear disappears when you are able to embrace all of life! Love and life moves us forward.

THE SOURCE OF JOY

The feeling that comes with being a co-worker with the force of love may be described as being in love with life. Anybody who has been in love with anything has tasted a little morsel of what it feels like when the connection with the Holy Spirit is made. And because of the infinite nature of love, the feeling gets better and better. Some connected people refer to that feeling as a throb of joy! Life definitely feels different when this joy starts seeping in.

My personal connection with the Holy Spirit started when a blue light began to appear at times when I was still and had my eyes closed. The more often I saw this blue light (which sometimes appeared as a blue star), the more relaxed I became towards everything. These days the blue light appears constantly when I stay still and close my eyes. When I see it, I can't help but have the feeling that everything is okay – and I am just happy to be allowed to be a part of the whole happening, happy to be alive.

I know the Earth is often referred to as the blue planet. So maybe the blue star or blue light represents the governing spirit or transformer of the Universal Spirit on Earth, a special guide who helps us to connect to Spirit and the real source of joy.

Perhaps this is the guide, teacher, or master that appeared when I was ready.

LETTING SPIRIT SHINE THROUGH

After a period of time in Boot Camp, human beings become polished enough for the light of God to start shining through them. All the so-called trials that a person goes through in life are apparently to get it ready to become such a source of light in the universe. However, to reflect light from the source, a person also needs to become transparent. This means an active and continuous vigilance in keeping oneself clean and polished.

How does a person stay clean? Primarily by being able to live in the moment. Life—which can be thought of as the light and sound of God—is always here in the nowness of the present, with everything that is alive. When we are ready, most of our attention remains on whatever is going on in the present. That is the meaning of focus. One of the reasons we are given the opportunity of being human is so we can learn how to tune into the ever-present flow of life.

When we have expectations, we are putting too much attention on the future. Blame and guilt put too much attention on the past. Too much attention on the past or the future takes away from being very efficient in the present. Since the future depends on the present, it stands to reason that when the present is formed well, the future can't help but be good. And when the future turns out well, it means the past was good. This makes it very important that we focus on making the present as good as possible. So basically, it all starts now! We are always in the cycle of time, which is like a circle. And in a circle, every spot is a beginning or an end, which means that it is never too late to stop or start anything.

Life brings the present around again every day. It is always given to you (because you have life), but you must be fully present to recognize the gift and be able to use it properly. All that is required for your presence is a normal mind and a pure heart. Then, one of these days, if you haven't already, you will become conscious of the gift of the present – and you will know your purpose in life. Apparently, that is when the real living begins! Before then, we bounce around in the dark, scratching and fighting, winning and losing – and that is okay too, for now.

BREATHING IN TRANQUILITY

C hange is the one thing we can all count on. So, any time is a good time to stop a bad habit and start a good one. Life is patient! And we are loved.

In fact, Life loves us so much that it made our heartbeat and our breathing automatic. I keep reminding myself that I have the opportunity to help Love keep me alive by breathing properly. Since my connection with the rest of the universe is through the air, every day, as often as I can remember, I make the effort to fill up my lungs to their capacity with air – which happens to be free of charge and easily available most of the time! Proper breathing also has a tendency to help the heart beat properly. So, as often as I can, I pay attention to my breathing! For me, this is a very good habit.

I also find that breathing properly and paying attention to the sound of my heartbeat helps me break through my chain of thoughts, so that I can focus more on the daily duties I need to perform to be of service to life as I work towards being selfless. Paradoxically, being selfless involves getting the imitation self, the ego, out of the way so that the real polished self can come through and be of service. This is part of being a conscious spiritual being.

And what is the point of becoming a conscious spiritual being? Wisdom, freedom and charity (or unconditional love) are the companions of every conscious spiritual being, but it also brings with it a beautiful sense of tranquility.

There is a saying that *"the poor want to be rich, the rich long for heaven, and the wise long for tranquility."* Tranquility – or peace beyond the realm of the mind – is one practical benefit that accompanies you in your daily living, once you begin walking in the world of Spirit. Until then, there is the company of anxiety. Before I became aware of my eternal side, I was filled with anxiety and uncertainty. Fear ruled my life. Time was of the essence and I was always glancing at my wrist watch. I was happily a slave to time, which only made me more anxious.

We are going to perform our daily duties regardless of whether we have anxiety or tranquility as our companion. I choose tranquility. In the meantime, anxiety will make sure that everyone eventually begins to walk the path to tranquility – so anxiety of itself is not a bad thing. Negativity does thrive on anxiety, though. Again, I choose tranquility.

Since humility is a basic requirement for an introduction to your Spirit self, the ego must also be transcended before the onset of tranquility. This makes sense when you realize that the ego is basically the anxious negative self which has yet to come to terms with its mortality and the reality that its source is Spirit, rather than a collection of flesh and bones. For this reason, I find that the act of learning to die daily also helps me get the ego or imitation self (and any past and future aberrations) out of the way, so that I can be with the fresh nature of the now! I do not want to miss the show anymore by being distracted by my past or my hopes for the future. I do my best to let go of both my past victories and defeats, and my aspirations for future wins and fears of future losses. It is not easy to do this, but every time I succeed, the energy and freshness I feel makes me want to give it a try again. It always brings positive change in my life.

It took me some time to become aware that change is the one thing I can count on – and that the only way I can painlessly and gracefully experience change is to let go of my thoughts and opinions about everything! It is very relaxing and invigorating when I succeed in going with the flow. It takes practice and patience but it is well worth it. Again, I have to keep reminding myself that I should be grateful for being allowed to be wherever I am on the circle of life, and that wherever I am is a good spot to start being consciously in tune with life and the universe, and start being happy. It is never too late to be happy!

BEING TRANSPARENT

To be able to receive and transmit light requires a certain amount of transparency. Whenever I feel like I am "filled with the exuberance of my own verbosity" – or slipping into the drama of life – I know I am not at my transparent best.

One key to transparency, I have found, is doing away with secrets in my life. I have never, ever wanted to be a part of anything secret. Secrecy only breeds misery. In fact, it is said that it takes seven secrets to guard one secret. What is a secret? A dark spot in a sea of light. It is just a matter of time before light engulfs all darkness! A secret society is then just a society that needs to be and is waiting to be enlightened. As far as I can understand, though, secrecy is for creepy-crawlers that are afraid of light, just like a band of cockroaches. They scatter when the light comes in.

We do ourselves a favour by not being a part of any secret. The idea is finally to be transparent, free and happy. A transparent person is the kind of person everybody wants as a friend. Who wants to be close to someone who is harbouring a lot of secrets? Who wants to be close to a creepy person? Maybe another creepy person! Like attracts like, so then if you want to be attracted to a transparent person, get busy making yourself transparent.

The universe is big. We are blessed with free will and the power to create, so we should pay attention to our thoughts and actions. I believe we end up creating our lives here and hereafter. We have the power and choice to steer our way towards goodness – or God, in a short form. Basically, we have the free will to carve out our happiness or misery.

ASKING FOR HELP

At some point, many of us reach a place in our lives when we ask, "Is that all there is?" Some call it a midlife crisis. Often, it is really an internal hunger for more. In my case, it had taken me 40 years to finally admit that I didn't have all the answers. After exhausting my mental resources, I finally remembered asked for help. As soon as I was ready, a long-time friend nonchalantly mentioned that they had learned that every Soul gets to a point where they need spiritual guidance, so I decided to try asking for spiritual guidance. I had no idea how to go about this simple project, though. I was too shy to ask my friend *how* to ask to be guided by Spirit. I suppose the simplicity of it was just too much for my sophisticated persona, my egotistical little self. So, I struck out of my own.

The first thing that came to my mind was: go to church. So off to church I went. My father was a Presbyterian minister, so I started with that. The nearest similar church I could find was a United Church in the neighbourhood. The minister was very warm and helpful. So was the congregation. I stayed with the church for awhile, but part of me still felt unsatisfied. It is hard to explain, but I knew I had to keep open for something more than what belonging to that good church was offering me. About that time, I ran into my old friend again and shared my experience of looking for spiritual guidance in church. The input I received from my friend this time was a bit of a shocker. Basically, I was left with the idea that I needed an actual spiritual guide, and that whenever I was indeed ready to dive into a more personal experience in spirituality, I would somehow meet that guide. Until then, I could only be patient, continue going about my daily duties – meeting my family, job, and social obligations – and trust that the spiritual hunger I felt inside me would lead me on in my quest.

My first "awakening" experiences happened in my dreams. I kept meeting different personalities in my dreams, all of whom hinted at the same idea: Your guide is as close to you as your heartbeat. This at least gave me an inkling that there was indeed something within me waiting to be communicated with. I then had a dream in which I was told that, if I spent some quiet time each day with my thoughts, I would soon have conscious contact with this inner guide, and that this guide had been with me, guiding me, all along though I had been unaware of it. I was told that becoming aware of and working with this inner guide of mine was going to lead me to my purpose on Earth.

I spent the next several years reading about all kinds of spiritual organizations and paths. Each day I also spent some time in quiet repose. I guess it was some kind of meditating. I was slowly coming to an awareness that I had a great and adventurous task ahead of me, to get and stay in conscious contact with something in myself that was, in turn, in touch with the life force. A strange thing then started to happen. I found that I was beginning to identify more and more with this thing within myself, while the "me" that started the whole process seemed to be falling away, like a shadow does when light engulfs it.

My dreams continued to be quite an exciting part of my life. Different individuals from my past, and others who were new to me, began participating in my dreams as some sort of spiritual guides or teachers. How can everybody I've ever been around be a teacher to me? I wondered. This was especially perplexing because I thought very little of some of them. I found this mind boggling since they all seemed to point out things that were helping me out in my daily living.

I had come across the idea before that everybody acts as a teacher and a student in life. Still, this was hard to accept because of my lack of respect and the position of judgment I held toward many of the people I had known. After all, I figured, it was not my fault that I had not yet met anybody I thought was perfect – including myself. I would eventually grow into the awareness that respect and non-judgment are two of the essential ingredients that come with working with the source of life, or God.

As the dreams continued, the most profound truths seemed to come from the most despicable people I had ever been blessed to know! What bothered me most about this was that, because of my resistance to these personalities, I knew I was not getting the full benefit of whatever truth was coming through them. What to do?

Then I saw a program on TV, where a certain spiritual leader was asked how a person could get in touch with their eternal self. The answer was, "Through daily practice!" I wondered what there was to practice. I had tuned into the program late and had obviously missed hearing the particular things that he had suggested were to be practiced. I was then advised in one of my dreams to try using my heart instead of my mind, for a change, and see how that experience felt.

A second dream experience then gave a bit of an insight into the difference between being from the heart and being from the mind. It was a bit of spiritual logic that went like this: The brain controls a biological entity. The mind controls the brain because the brain is not quite capable of dealing with the magnetic field around the biological entity. The mind of itself is like a machine – an etheric machine. The heart is also a machine, but it is in direct touch with the hand of the Source of life, which is love. It is well known in all cultures that the heart is a source of love. It serves as a reminder of Life's love for us, because it beats automatically both in sleep and in waking life. It also represents unconditional love because it keeps on beating even when we turn away from God. Even those who say there is no God are still taken care of and benefit from an automatic heartbeat. Therefore, when a person begins to act and think from the heart, that person begins to practice working with love and starts being prepared to become the likeness of love.

Soon, my experiment with working from the heart began. It wasn't long after I started acting and thinking from the heart that I realized there was a fringe benefit that came with learning to work with love. The main point was that as you begin filling yourself with love, you experience a definite increase in peace and joy. I was always a pretty happy person, but now I realized that I could be even happier!

Since every Soul is on their way home to God, it is nice to be able to say that there is joy waiting, in the end, for everybody. I realized that the simple fact that we are allowed to be conscious beings means we are loved. This awareness of and thankfulness for the gift of life itself has been the foundation of my basic gratitude practice. I am even beginning to find it amusing when I come across a person who is complaining about the works of life, because I realize they are forgetting that they have been "allowed" to be – simply to exist – by the grace of God.

It is said that a wise person sees everything as if they are seeing it for the first time. That's how grateful a wise person is for being allowed to be a conscious entity and given an opportunity to be a co-worker of the life force. They have become like little children, and are able to be aware of heaven. This is another benefit of working and being from the heart. The art of gratitude helps a person act and think from the highest viewpoint they have earned at that time.

For me, being from the heart was the beginning of falling in love with life. It has been a continuous process of coming to life, waking up, becoming full of light (I was blind but now I see!). I realize that everything is in its proper order. The more aware or conscious I become of this, the less anxiety (a product of fear, not love) is present in my day to day life. It has taken daily practice for this calm knowingness to penetrate and help replace fear with love in my system, but now my enthusiasm for every part and phase of my life is on the increase. This is what I have always wanted – to regain a childlike attitude towards life.

There is no feeling power can offer than can even come close to the feeling of being in love with life. If you watch children happily at play you can get a slight idea of how you will feel when you practice keeping in touch with your eternal self – enough to fall in love with it! And this, as I say, is the beginning of falling in love with all life. We do indeed have to be like little children before we can taste the "air" of heaven. Before children begin to learn the ways of the world, (i.e. develop the protective survival gear of the ego), they are usually in touch with their eternal self, and so are capable of exuding joy most of the time.

With time, at the end of the purification process, everybody will experience this joy and taste heaven – even while still in a body! The source of love has this waiting for everybody.

THE AMUSEMENT PARK OF LIFE

I once had a dream of being in an amusement park as a child. It seemed that I was at the end of my stay. I was done with all the rides. I'd had it with the sweet and sour and the pain and pleasure of the roller coasters and all the wonderful thrills the park offered. At the end of every thrill, I remember feeling sick to my stomach and vowing to myself that I would not even look at another ride. But then the feeling would subside and I would feel myself drawn to another ride, and then another. This had gone on for what seemed like days and days.

Then, for a reason beyond my mental understanding, I stopped feeling drawn to the rides anymore. I could still appreciate the thrills they gave! I even chose to go on some rides to see if those thrills were still there, but there was a difference now. I still found them attractive but I wasn't drawn to them anymore. It reminded me of a saying of "being in this world but not of it" – being sort of detached from life but still participating in it. Strangely, in this detached state, I enjoyed the rides even more.

It was a strange feeling! I wondered how it was that I could now enjoy the rides in the amusement park even more, after I knew for sure I had had enough of them. For a while, I found myself going back on every ride, over and over again, just to make sure I was done. Then, suddenly, I realized that there really was no thrill anymore. Instead, the joy was in knowing how the rides worked and especially in knowing that I was not only being allowed to be on the rides but – even more importantly – being allowed to learn how they worked.

Then came a brief period of emptiness when I realized that I did not really care to go on the rides anymore. This emptiness, or sadness of a sort, went on for awhile until I looked up (beyond myself) and saw some friends standing in line for a ride I had just come off. The childish enthusiasm on their little faces sent a jolt of joy and peace rushing through me. I spent what seemed like endless days just being around friends who were waiting in line to go on rides. Their enthusiasm for the future, for the next ride they would go on, seemed to give me joy and some weird feeling of peace.

Then came the time when I began seeing friends who were feeling sick to their stomachs at the end of their rides. Sadness slowly started to creep into my system again. I found myself sharing my experience at the park with these friends – and this sharing opened the door for more joy to seep into me again, especially when I saw how hearing my story made their pain go away.

Eventually I learned how to operate and fix rides! I even apprenticed and became in charge of a whole amusement park – after I realized what they were for! Then it was time to go home. This time, I returned home willingly, instead of having to be dragged out of the park when I had grown into another phase in my life where there were more things to do than just being in the amusement park.

I'd had a glimpse of Soul's purpose on Earth! Correction: I had been allowed a glimpse of Soul's purpose on Earth.

This dream ties in with the idea that karma and reincarnation purify and shape Soul into the likeness of God. The purpose of the grinding wheel of karma is to prepare Souls to fall in love with life, to align Souls with the workings of the love force. And what is life? Life is your presence! So, you get a better and better view of yourself as you go along. As the saying goes, you end up experiencing yourself! And God experiences itself through you.

If we look at the gift of life like a ticket to an amusement park, what do we do after we are allowed into the park?

1. Learn the rules (childhood, innocence, school)
2. Continue on with the experience (adulthood, leaving paradise)
3. Leave the park (old age, detachment, wisdom – if all goes well)

This process is sometimes referred to as "Divine Play" – as in being at play in the fields of the Lord, perhaps, or as in playing in the amusement park of life. There are exciting times at the amusement park – round and round you go. We get to know all the rides of life. We get to know how they run. We get to know how to fix them when they break. And, as we mature, we get to be guides who lead fresh Souls around the park. Maturing means understanding your role.

Eventually, you learn that you are being put through everything you are going through so that you can become an individualized, unique likeness of God. A star? Maybe so. How many stars are possible? As many as you can imagine – and you are destined to be one of them. To learn to just be! And when you can help other Souls discover it all, then you are prepared to help create. Create what? Whatever! Sound exciting yet??

If this is not an incentive to carry on as an "allowed" conscious being, then I do not know what else can motivate a Soul.

ARMS OF THE DIVINE

There seem to be two basic stages to the spiritual journey:

Stage 1: Realizing that there is an eternal part of you that is waiting patiently to be realized or woken up to and put into practice. Realized means to be made real. Maybe this is what is referred to as Self-Realization.

Stage 2: When that self is realized to be a part of something larger – God– then comes the onset of God Realization.

Things really begin to get exciting when you realize that IT (God, Love, the Force) has been with you all the time, waiting to be realized. Since that which is being realized is part of an eternal source, you begin to slowly partake in and of eternity. That is IT!!

You were created in the image of God. It is said that everybody is important because the universe experiences itself through the actions and thoughts of every individual. It is our purpose to become "recovered" individualized images of God. The result of the whole process is to create an arm of the divine. An individual is only required to help with the process. It is in the interest of the Divine Source that each investment (and that includes you!) become a successfully working arm.

Thy kingdom come, Thy will be done...

When we do God's will, we are in the Divine Moment or, in other words, in God's kingdom.

TAILOR-MADE TIMING

The process of realizing your eternal side will unveil life for you, slowly and thoroughly, efficiently and inexorably as the mill or wheel of God, in a way that is individually tailored just for you. Passages through the wheel lead to slowly becoming one with the force (God). We take on the nature of love; we slowly fall into love's way; we fall in love (with life).

How long does this process take? As long as necessary! Eternity promises an infinite number of growth opportunities and experiences. What can provide more enthusiasm for life than knowing that each new day provides a chance to experience a new aspect of life? The peak of every mountain we climb marks the bottom of the next higher one. Often, there seem to be heavy, dark clouds hanging around just below the peak of each mountain apex, making it look paradoxically far away while so near. This just tests our spiritual stamina and faith needed for the next level. The tests make sure we have earned our passage onward and higher. And in this whole training process, love makes all the difference.

The best training I ever received was from a loving source. I remember how our high school athletic team took a turn for the better when we got a new coach who we knew cared about us. We even enjoyed the more rigorous training schedule that he put us through. The previous coach had believed in using fear and control to train us. Though his training methods were not as strenuous as those of the new coach, his sessions were very uncomfortable – almost painful.

Are We There Yet?

Can it be that when we realize that we are loved, life (and this includes passing through the wheel of karma) can be a totally different experience? It seems that this is what our loving source has in store for each and every created Soul. *"In my father's house, there are many mansions"*. There is room for every created Soul. And everybody will get there eventually.

BECOMING THE NATURE OF LOVE

What God has put in place, nothing can change it. You are loved. If you can read or hear this message, and even if you can't read or hear this, your Creator saw fit to create you, and only the Creator can take it away from you. Whatever you are prepared to do for what you love pales in comparison to what the source of life (Love) is prepared to do for you. So "seek ye first the kingdom of God and all will be added unto you". And take comfort, for you need not look too far: the kingdom of God is within you.

How do we go about seeking the kingdom within us?

1. by learning to love ourselves;
2. by learning to treat others the way we would like to be treated;
3. by learning to be love.

When you finally start falling in love with life, the first thing that happens to you is that you begin to love yourself. How does this happen? When we fall in love, we get filled with love. We become love. We are love! This is also how you begin to love yourself. You treat yourself as a loving mother treats her children. Then you behave like love behaves, and you begin to learn how to pass on love. This is how you came to be. You are the result of love being passed on. Everything in existence is the result of love's extension, of love being passed on. This all sounds very simple, and it is simple when we learn to keep it simple.

The qualities we embrace when we become aware that we are love and begin to love ourselves include patience, tolerance, enthusiasm, perseverance, respect, non-judgment, honesty, detachment, forgiveness, gratitude, generosity, and compassion. These qualities of love become our nature. Then we are able to see life from a higher viewpoint which comes from the higher nature of love.

PURIFICATION

When you are working and playing in the garden, getting dirty is just a natural part of the whole happening. Taking a shower or bath afterward is also a part of the experience, so that we are fresh and clean for the next part of the day. A similar idea applies to Soul's maturation process. Spiritual maturity is the result of the ongoing purification process of life, which Love provides to clean us up.

What is there to clean up? What is it that interferes with Soul's link up with divinity? Self – that's what! The false self, the ego, that same little self that is self-created for survival on the physical plane. It is the hard-covering that is there to protect the seed of the inner self. This splitting apart of the ego can be uncomfortable if a person does not learn to let go – and let God! Perhaps that is why the ego seems to struggle when the real self emerges to take over.

The purification process includes all the hardships that we face. Diseases and illnesses also seem to be an integral part of the purification of Soul. In fact, an illness in the physical body can be a healing program for Soul – a means of waking us up to our own divine nature and clearing away anything that keeps us from shining.

Every obstacle we face has the potential to be a stepping stone or a stumbling block. It is our choice. For a patient and all-knowing custodian or parent, it does not matter what choice their charge makes. One choice (Plan A) will introduce a person to a higher point of view on how to keep following and distributing light and love. The other choice (Plan B – which happens to have all the ingredients for a little bowl of misery: stumble, maybe fall, some level of discomfort) will eventually help a person learn to go with Plan A. It is all a part of Soul's education, purification, and refinement.

At any point in the cycle, you can remember to ask for help because every point in a circle is as good a starting point as it is a finishing point (interesting point!). There are circles of cycles, and cycles of circles. Round and around they go – where they end nobody knows. This is the phenomenon referred to as the wheel of karma. Someone I know even refers to it as "the spring board to eternity". That strikes me as a nice approach to the circles and cycles of the karmic wheel. It sounds like Love's point of view on the ongoing purification program for Soul. Every experience teaches us something about our eternal nature.

LIVING FROM THE INSIDE OUT

The human self is like a lantern that needs to be cleaned off so that the light within it can really shine. Then it can be used by the person and, on a larger scale, can help light up this planet and spread love to it. The cleaning up starts from the inside, closest to the light, so that one can see what needs cleaning. The more layers are taken off from the inside out, the bigger and brighter the light becomes. With enough cleaning and enough light, a person becomes enlightened – filled with light and love.

This is a return to our true nature. You see, since the Kingdom of God (Heaven) exists within each person, this means that a part of God is within each person. Each person is basically love. Extending love, or passing love on, is a God-like quality. The more love you pass on, the more love comes into you from the source of love. Sounds simple, but is not easy to do. The main obstacles that block this process of passing on love are those pesky five passions – anger, greed, lust, undue attachment to material things, and last but not the least, vanity – which are the stuff of the ego. That's what we are cleaning up.

Leading life from the inside out requires working with the light, working with love. Love and light sort of come together and become one and the same when you get to know them well. They are branches of the same tree. Might they even be the same force in different forms? I believe so.

As you remove the layers from inside, you open your heart and allow the love that is bottled up in there begin to flow out, like it has been waiting to do. It is the nature of love to expand; that is how creation came to be. And our purpose as individual entities is to continue with the program and keep the love flowing! As you pass love on, more love fills you up. Hence the paradox – learning to love yourself involves learning to love something outside yourself. To get love, you must give it. That's just how it works. Life gives back what you put in. Serve life or nature and it will serve you back.

REPETITIONS

C onstant repetition is a basic modus operandi in life. Even the
planets and heavenly bodies keep repeating their movements,
over and over. The Earth does the same. Perhaps, like the Earth, our
bodies can also be considered heavenly bodies. It certainly helps me
to keep reminding myself that I am a spiritual being in a temporary
earthly body. And of course, as long as we have bodies, we need to
take care of them. Day in, day out. Repetitions of our duties and the
things we need to do.

We also need to put our attention on our basic support system
as often as possible, so we can flow with life. What is our basic
support system? It is life. And what is the essence of life? It is our
own presence, that quiet inner self. It is advisable to contact this inner
self often, as often as daily. Why daily? Because days are the basic
repetitions of life on Earth. We need to do something on a daily basis
to bring into reality that which is securely placed inside of us. This
means making time each day to communicate with the eternal part
of us. How? Put aside some quiet time. Follow your breathing. Pay
attention to your heartbeat. Pay attention to the inner sounds that
are constantly present. Remember that you are loved.

Knowing you are loved is the first stage. The second stage is to
learn to love yourself. This stage is arrived at after the continuous
practice of getting in touch with your eternal self, within your heart.
Nobody can come between you and yourself unless you allow them.
Souls who are in touch with their divine, eternal selves also don't get

into a master-slave circle of karma (which is very uncomfortable to say the least) because they are operating from love.

The learning curve of life seems to be composed of repetitions of the practice of receiving and spreading love in one form or another. I have found that the practice of gratitude infuses enthusiasm into the continuous cycles and circles of learning. Without the constant practice of gratitude, the learning curve of life can be dulled by the infusion of vanity and pride, which are two of the cutting fronts of egotism – every Soul's personal agent of sensual bondage. Without gratitude, we may forget to truly live and settle for simply existing, plodding along. Forgetting to live is the same thing as unknowingly being effect of life and just letting it all happen to you. We can also let impatience slide in and interfere with our rhythm.

Apparently, there is a lot of repetition in the process of purification. You either go up or down, move on or go back. Use it or lose it. Constant vigilance eventually leads to spiritual vision – a sense of the works of love. Eventually Love replaces fear. Light replaces darkness. Until then, repetition promotes the idea of practice. It seems to take constant practice to stay in touch with our divine selves, and to fall in love and stay in love with life. First, we're in love with life, then out of love with life, the heart opens, the heart closes. The cycles repeat over and over again. If your heart is open and you are in love with life 51% of the time, you're doing well! However, patience and constant practice help you earn your level of love every day – until you can assume your position as Soul every waking moment.

Does it ever stop? The wise ones keep saying that the learning and mastering process never ends. However, they seem to say this with enthusiasm and with a "looking forward to more learning" gleam in their eye, which gives one hope!

ARE WE THERE YET?

So, are we there yet? Well, really, there is nowhere to go. That which we are aiming to reach is always with us; we are just not aware of it yet, but we will be. We are given the gift of consciousness as human beings. Consciousness is awareness, and the reason we are "allowed" to be human is so that we can eventually become aware that we have the spark of God invested in us. When we become aware of and get in touch with this spark, then we are "there". We become conscious that "there" is always here, now. The search is then over and anywhere we are is then home to us!

The real living and the fun begins when we are aware of being a part of God, and when we begin to consciously work with It. I guess that is what is described as being a co-worker with God. Every physical body that we are given becomes a vehicle to be used by us under Its direction. We are Its agents, agents of love! Ever since I was a kid, I have wanted to be an agent of something supremely good, so this suits me just fine. There is no need for personal agendas anymore. All personal needs are already met. It is our desires that keep us distracted and unaware of the continuing presence of God within everything. It is our desires that make us unaware of our true selves and our potential. Desires limit our minds to the domain of the senses for a period of time, so that we can get to know ourselves as children of God and learn humility and gratitude.

It never ceases to amaze me just how intricately Love is woven into all creation! It is behind everything that occurs.

Are We There Yet?

I am now aware that the idea of being born in sin was just a product of fear, which was considered necessary in order to control the out-of-control beast that desires can turn a human into. The source of life, which is love, has no need to push its children into sin for them to recognize themselves as part of It. That story mistakenly makes it look like the source of life is evil, rather than love. Of course, we all have the free will to choose to believe and be whatever we want, but I know I would not want any of my children or friends to perish – and my capacity to love is miniscule compared to the love that I am aware of that keeps my heart beating. So, I choose to believe that everybody will get "there", in time. If I am allowed to get there, surely everybody will end up in joy!

We are loved more than we can even imagine. I am beginning to get it – that love is behind everything, that love is the main force in creation, and eventually every person will wake up to this reality and do themselves a favour by consciously working with it, because each person and thing is created and sustained by it.

Knowing that I am loved, I am learning to love myself more. I need to love myself before I can be a centre for distributing love – a mini transmitter of love! Can this be our main purpose, our destiny? Can it be this simple? Yes! Isn't it nice to know that you are sitting on an infinite supply of joy.

So, are we there yet? There is nowhere to go. Where we are trying to get to is always here with us – now. All we need to do is to open up to it, and be it!

There is a beautiful quote from Rumi that sums it all up: *"You are soul and you are love, not a sprite or an angel or a human being. You are a Godman-womanGod-manGod-Godwoman. No more questions now as to what it is we are doing here."*

– FINI –

Endnote:

1. *A Year with Rumi*, May 2

Printed in the United States
By Bookmasters